Ben Jonson

VOLPONE

Notes by Douglas Duncan

MA (OXON), Ph.D (ABERDEEN)
Professor of English, McMaster University

LONGMAN
YORK PRESS

YORK PRESS
Immeuble Esseily, Place Riad Solh, Beirut

ADDISON WESLEY LONGMAN LIMITED
Edinburgh Gate, Harlow,
Essex CM20 2JE, England
Associated companies, branches and representatives
throughout the world

© Librairie du Liban 1980

First published 1980
Eleventh impression 1996

ISBN 0-582-02317-3

Produced by Longman Singapore Publishers Pte Ltd
Printed in Singapore

Contents

Part 1: Introduction   *page* 5
    Volpone and Jonson's earlier career   5
    Volpone and classical literary tradition   7
    Volpone and popular tradition   7
    Religious and philosophical background   8
    The Venetian setting   9
    The Globe Theatre   10
    A note on the text   11

Part 2: Summaries   12
    A general summary   12
    Detailed summaries   14

Part 3: Commentary   40
    Themes and morals   40
    Structure   44
    Characters   49
    Imagery   53
    Rhetoric and irony   56

Part 4: Hints for study   59
    Reading the play   59
    Preparing for examinations   59
    Answering examination questions   61

Part 5: Suggestions for further reading   68

The author of these notes   70

Part 1

Introduction

Volpone is recognised as one of the greatest comedies in the English language, and of all Ben Jonson's plays is the most frequently acted today. Anyone who has been lucky enough to see it on the stage will understand why. It is a fast-moving farce packed full of situations which are as funny to us as they were to its first audience in 1606, a satire on the greed of money-mad societies which is even more relevant now than in the seventeenth century. But its mixture of humour and serious satire, so obvious in the theatre, is harder to appreciate from the text alone. To experience a play by reading the text is almost as difficult as to experience a film by reading a film-script. In reading plays we must use our imagination even more than in reading novels: we must *see* what is happening on stage; we must *hear* the speeches; we must *sense* how the actors manipulate the feelings of their audience. A main aim of this book is to help the reader to experience *Volpone* in such ways.

This will be attempted in the scene-by-scene summaries in Part 2, which should be used when working through the text for the first time. Then, in Part 3, we shall draw on our experience to discuss the art of the author and the themes he explores. Finally, Part 4 will give practical advice to the student who is preparing to write essays or exam-answers. Difficult words and references in the text are explained in the Notes and Glossary at the end of the summary of each scene in Part 2, but for further help of this kind it is expected that the student will turn to the notes and glossary of whatever edition is being used (see p. 11). Editions also give factual information about Jonson's life and other works. This introduction covers background topics which are needed to understand *Volpone*.

Volpone and Jonson's earlier career

Jonson was about thirty-two when he wrote *Volpone*. He seems to have regarded it as the kind of brilliant achievement which is sometimes the reward of a long, hard apprenticeship. He hints at this in the Prologue (lines 11–18) where he claims to have written *Volpone* in five weeks instead of the year which his critics teased him for usually spending on each play. Believing that art is most successful when it comes to seem natural and effortless, he probably saw his whole earlier career as leading up to this triumph. All his life he had had to work hard. His father had died before his birth in 1573, and he had been brought up in a poor London household. Although he was lucky to get several years of excellent free education in Latin and Greek at Westminster School, he did not go on to university but instead worked as a bricklayer for his stepfather and served as a soldier in the Netherlands before getting a job as an actor and starting to write plays. The clearest proof of Jonson's courage and determination is that between the age of about seventeen and twenty-five, when he was leading a rough-and-tumble life, he managed to continue his reading of classical authors and establish himself as a 'scholar-poet' who could win the respect of some of the best-educated men of his time, such men as the poet John Donne and his former schoolmaster William Camden.

The guiding ideals which Jonson formed in those years were, first, that the poet (even when he wrote for a popular medium like the stage) must always be a careful craftsman, basing his work on study of the classical masters; secondly, that the poet's task was not only to please his public but also to teach it how to live. These two ideals were eloquently stated by Sir Philip Sidney in his *Defence of Poetry*, published in 1595. Neither of them would have seemed strange to Shakespeare, who was nine years older than Jonson and had begun writing plays only a few years earlier, but Jonson adopted them much more deliberately, posing as the 'professor' among contemporary dramatists and always tending to be suspicious of Shakespeare's crowd-pleasing methods and his disregard of classical principles. Jonson did not believe in imitating ancient authors slavishly; he thought they should be followed 'as guides, not commanders', and all his early works were bold experiments in adapting their techniques to modern conditions. But he never wavered in his belief that plays should be carefully-composed works of art containing a strong moral message.

In the three comedies which came before *Volpone* (called 'comical satires') Jonson had irritated audiences and made himself ridiculous by preaching his messages openly through characters who denounce the folly and corruption of the times. Stung by the failure of these plays, he wrote a learned tragedy on the downfall of the Roman tyrant Sejanus which also failed badly on the stage. Though *Sejanus* was admired by his educated friends, especially when published in 1605 with a full list of its sources in the Roman historians, Jonson was too much a man of the theatre to be content with the admiration of scholars alone. In *Volpone* he satisfied all tastes, including his own. Making everyone laugh, he also presented a devastating picture of human nature at its worst, challenging all those who laughed to consider why they were laughing at all. The success of the play, both with the mass audience of the Globe Theatre in the spring of 1606 and with the academic audiences at Oxford and Cambridge in the following summer, showed that Jonson had found a formula for bridging the gap between learned and popular art.

Volpone and classical literary tradition

When we talk of *Volpone* as a 'learned' comedy, we think primarily of its debts to the classics. The most important of these are:

1. Structure. In constructing his plot Jonson deliberately followed many of the 'rules' for the writing of comedy based by Renaissance theorists on the *Poetics* of the Athenian philosopher Aristotle (384–322 BC) and on the plays of the Roman comic dramatist Terence (195–159 BC) (see below, pp. 44–6).

2. Characterisation. Jonson's method of portraying characters, more as 'types' than as individuals, also shows the influence of Renaissance theory based on classical example (see below, pp. 49–50).

3. Plot-sources. The basic situation of a rich man flattered by a 'parasite' and courted by 'friends' who hope to inherit his wealth reflects the practice of legacy-hunting described by the Roman satirists Horace (65–8 BC), Juvenal and Petronius (1st century AD) and by the Syrian Greek author Lucian (2nd century AD). In some stories, as in *Volpone*, the hunters are encouraged and then tricked by their victim.

4. Allusions. The play is full of references (open or concealed) to classical literature, history and myth: for instance, the entertainment offered to Volpone in Act I and Volpone's speeches to Celia in Act III. Since most of the references are to Roman civilisation in its period of decadence, Jonson implies that the modern world of the play is similarly decadent.

Volpone and popular tradition

Spectators who knew nothing of the classical world found familiar associations in *Volpone*:

1. Animal fable. Stories about animals told to illustrate a moral had been written down by the Greek fabulist Aesop (6th century BC) and other ancient writers but were orally transmitted in Jonson's day and known to all sectors of society. Jonson chiefly uses the story of The Fox and the Birds. The fox pretends to be dying, attracts the birds that eat dead flesh, and grabs them when they come close. In Italian, Volpone means 'big fox'; Voltore, Corbaccio, Corvino mean 'vulture', 'nasty old crow', 'fine young raven'. Mosca is the 'fly' who buzzes round the body to attract the birds; he is the parasite which feeds off the host-animal while it lives and hopes to feed off its corpse when it dies. We must also remember that the fox, often called Reynard, was one of the most popular figures in European folklore. Clever and resourceful, a skilled actor and disguiser and hypocrite, he was enjoyed as a humorous character but he was also seen as greedy and sinister, a type of the devil capturing men's souls with his tricks. Volpone is all these things. This leads us to:

2. Morality drama. Still remembered in Jonson's day, the popular medieval 'morality play' dramatised the Christian idea of God and Satan, good and evil, fighting for the soul of man. Characters in these plays were allegorical; that is, they usually represented virtues or vices. Traditionally, vice-characters were shown as dangerously attractive. Like Reynard the Fox and Volpone, they appealed to the audience by being lively and humorous, enjoying the pleasures of the world. Only in the end were they shown to be foolish, because it is always foolish to fight against the power of God. Virtue always triumphed in morality drama, but the good characters were not superficially attractive like the bad ones. Spiritual goodness is not clever, does not disguise itself, does not make jokes. We should remember this in considering the characters of Celia ('heavenly woman') and Bonario ('good man'). *Volpone* is not a simple morality play, but the audience was sometimes tempted to think that it was.

Religious and philosophical background

It is not necessary to be a seventeenth-century Christian to be shocked by the values of Volpone's world. We all agree that human beings *ought* not to behave like animals, *ought* not to worship gold, *ought* not to spend their lives acting parts to deceive others. But in doing these things Jonson's characters were violating standards which had greater authority then than now. Christians believed that man had been created by God with the gift of reason to enable him to rule over the animals and to control his own animal appetites. Reason could show him the difference between good and evil: if he used it well and chose good, he rose on the 'ladder of creation' toward God and his angels; if he used it badly to further his appetites, he became worse than an animal and was dragged down by Satan. Even more precious than the gift of reason was the gift of an immortal soul. Man's main task on earth was to purify his soul from worldly corruption so that after his death he could return it to God in heaven. Christ taught that wealth made it difficult for a man to get to heaven (*Matthew* 19:24), because the love of worldly things conflicts with the soul's desire to come closer to God. 'Ye cannot serve God and mammon' (*Luke* 16:13). These basic Christian ideas underlie *Volpone*. So also does the teaching of Stoic philosophers such as Seneca about the need to cultivate the 'self'. An individual should strive to regulate and perfect his character, and should then remain true to it, never disguising or altering it for the sake of temporary advantage. Only Celia and Bonario among Jonson's characters cultivate the self in this way.

But Jonson knew that these standards were seriously challenged in his time. The essence of what we call the Renaissance was the re-birth of man's interest in fulfilling his potentialities *in this world*, no longer valuing his life merely as preparation for eternity. Reason could not be restricted to the task of teaching man to live well and to save his soul; it had also to be applied to every kind of art and science. Immortality was something which men hoped to win through the fame of their achievements on earth. Wealth could be valued because it encouraged the creation of great works of architecture, painting, sculpture, literature—all the ways in which human genius can express itself. And a quality which came to be highly prized was versatility: the ability of an individual to play many different roles with success.

Obviously Jonson was himself a man of the Renaissance, in sympathy with all these ideals. Like other creative artists, he drew inspiration from discovering the man-centred civilisation of the ancient world, which had to be reconciled with God-centred Christian teaching. Like other playwrights (Marlowe, Shakespeare), he used the stage to dramatise conflicts between religious and humanistic values. *Volpone* is not an *attack* on the latter—indeed it celebrates some of the best qualities of the Renaissance mind: energy, subtlety, inventiveness, delight in splendour. But (like Shakespeare's *King Lear*, which was written at about the same time) it shows what happens to society when old religious values are replaced and almost forgotten.

The Venetian setting

If Jonson wanted to challenge English audiences, why did he set his play in Venice? Though he had never been there, he gathered information about it from published accounts and from his Italian friend John Florio (1553?–1625), and was careful to give accurate descriptions of its society, its buildings, its customs, its government. This concern for

accuracy was typical of Jonson the scholar, but it does not conceal that
he was mainly interested in Venice as a symbol. A city which had long
ago gained fabulous wealth as a trading-centre, it was already beginning its slow decline into the splendid, crumbling museum we know
today. Though it was still a centre of sophisticated Renaissance culture,
Jonson continually stresses its decadence—greedy and pleasure-loving
citizens, 'mountebank' scholars, corruptible lawyers—making it a
symbol of the godless materialism which he feared was overtaking his
own London. And behind Venice is the larger symbol of Italy, birth-
place of the Renaissance, where Englishmen saw that humanistic
values had been pushed to threatening extremes. Two sixteenth-century
Italian writers (casually mentioned in the play) sum up the nature of
this threat. Pietro Aretino (1492–1556), who had lived in Venice, was a
satirist who was thought to have debased literature by catering to the
lowest tastes of his readers for obscenity and pornography. The other,
more significant, is the Florentine statesman Niccolò Machiavelli
(1469–1527). In his *Prince* and *Discourses*, political treatises, Machiavelli had discussed government, not as the religious exercise of power
delegated by God, but as the practical science of imposing one's will on
other people. His assumption that the man most likely to succeed in
society is the boldest and cleverest and most unscrupulous, the one who
can best adapt himself to changing conditions, was the basis of Jonson's
satiric vision of a ruthlessly competitive society in *Volpone*.

The Globe Theatre

The background topics we have so far summarised are important to us
only because they contributed to a *play*, a play which was written with a
special kind of theatre in view. Elizabethan 'public' theatres like the
Globe were circular wooden structures, open to the sky in the centre. A
large rectangular stage, about six feet high, jutted out into the central
arena. Around it on three sides, looking up at the actors, the poorer
class of citizens sat or stood; while those who had paid more for ad-
mission sat in covered galleries, almost completely encircling the stage
and looking down on it, the most expensive seats being those at the
sides which were closest to the actors. At the back of the stage were two
doors through which the actors entered; between these a curtained
structure could be erected if the play required it; and above was a gallery where actors could appear to look down on the stage (as when
Celia appears at a 'window' in Act II of *Volpone*).

The Globe could hold up to 3,000 spectators, who were drawn from
all social classes and must have been crowded very closely together,

since the total diameter of the building was only one hundred feet. The closeness to each other of the social groups in the audience, and the closeness of all the spectators to the stage, should always be remembered. The actor, standing mid-stage, was directly in contact with the whole of his world. The audience, too, focused on the actor as its representative, seeing the play as a reflection of itself and its concerns.

This contact was especially valuable to Jonson who as satirist aimed to manipulate his public and to show it an unflattering reflection of its values. We can imagine the opening of *Volpone*. After the Prologue, a huge screened bed is pushed out into the centre of the stage from the curtained area at the rear. Volpone emerges and says 'Good morning to the day,' perhaps stretching himself and walking round the stage to make contact with the audience. Then he moves back to the curtained area and tells Mosca to 'open the shrine'. Jonson's Londoners watch as their representative kneels to worship his gold.

A note on the text

Volpone was first published in 1607, with a dedication and prefatory epistle addressed to the Universities of Oxford and Cambridge. It was later reprinted, with minor changes, in the 1616 folio volume of Jonson's *Works*.

Modern editions are numerous. Large libraries may contain the complete *Ben Jonson*, edited by Herford and Simpson, Oxford University Press, Oxford, 1925–52: introduction to *Volpone* in Volume II, text in Volume V, notes in Volume IX. Another edition which also prints the text in the original spelling is edited by Jay L. Halio, in the Fountainwell Drama Series, Oliver & Boyd, Edinburgh, 1968. Easier to read are modern-spelling editions by Jonas A. Barish, A.H.M. Publishing Corporation, Northbrook, Illinois, 1959; Alvin B. Kernan, Yale University Press, New Haven, 1962; David Cook, Methuen, London, 1962; Michael Jamieson in *Ben Jonson: Three Comedies*, Penguin Books, Harmondsworth, 1966; Philip Brockbank, New Mermaid series, Benn, London, 1968. Others exist, and this book may be used in conjunction with any of them, but the text and line-references given here are those of Brockbank. Students should note that some editions (for example, Cook's) abandon Jonson's practice of marking a new scene where the entry of new characters changes the focus of interest. Thus Act I (in which the action is continuous) is printed as a single scene by Cook though it is divided into five scenes by Jonson and most modern editors.

Part 2

Summaries
of VOLPONE

General summary

Act I: Volpone, a rich gentleman or 'magnifico' of Venice, schemes to get richer by pretending to be near death so that his friends will bring him valuable gifts in the hope of being named as his heir. He is aided in his plans by Mosca, his flattering servant or 'parasite'. After watching an entertainment (written by Mosca and acted by a dwarf, a eunuch and a hermaphrodite), Volpone receives visits from Voltore, a lawyer; Corbaccio, a deaf old gentleman; and Corvino, a young merchant. At the end of the act Volpone learns from Mosca that Corvino is the jealous husband of a beautiful wife, and he determines to see her.

Act II: Two English visitors to Venice, the clever young Peregrine and the foolish knight Sir Politic Would-Be, watch a Venetian 'mountebank', Scoto of Mantua, as he tries to sell a magical ointment. This is Volpone in disguise, who has set up his platform under the window of the beautiful Celia. She appears, but Corvino arrives and drives off the mountebank with blows. Mosca then visits Corvino with the news that the doctors have prescribed a cure for his sick master: a young woman must be found to sleep with him. Eager to impress Volpone, Corvino offers his wife, and tells Celia that they have been invited to a feast at Volpone's house.

Act III: On his way home Mosca meets Bonario, Corbaccio's son, and promises to hide him where he can overhear his father disinheriting him. Volpone is visited by Sir Politic Would-Be's wife, who is also interested in his money, but her chattering tongue is more than he can bear. Mosca, on his return, gets rid of her by saying he has seen her husband in a gondola with a courtesan. Corvino and Celia arrive sooner than expected, so Bonario is sent off to read in the gallery while waiting for his father. In a long scene Volpone attempts to seduce Celia; finally, when he is about to rape her, Bonario rushes in to the rescue and takes Celia away, promising to bring a lawsuit against Volpone. Faced with disaster, Mosca must think quickly. Corbaccio arrives, followed by Voltore who is suspicious of Corbaccio's intentions. Mosca tells the old man that his son had meant to kill him, thus strengthening his determination to disinherit Bonario in favour of

Volpone. Then Mosca persuades Voltore that this plan is meant to benefit *him*, so that he can inherit two fortunes (Corbaccio's as well as Volpone's). So the lawyer agrees to defend Volpone against the charge of rape.

Act IV: Lady Would-Be finds her husband conversing with Peregrine and assumes that the latter is the courtesan in disguise. Mosca arrives and promises to show her the real courtesan, if she will go with him to the law-court. In court, Voltore argues that Bonario and Celia are secret lovers who have brought a false charge against Volpone; he claims that Bonario meant to murder both Volpone and his father out of spite at being disinherited. Corbaccio gives evidence against his son, and Corvino against his wife. Then Lady Would-Be identifies Celia as the courtesan who had seduced her husband. Finally, Volpone is carried in to court, a helpless and speechless invalid. The judges cannot believe that he was capable of rape. Bonario and Celia are sent off to· prison to await sentencing.

Act V: Volpone plans to push his triumph further. He spreads news of his death, makes out a will in favour of Mosca, and then watches from behind a curtain as Voltore, Corbaccio, Corvino and Lady Would-Be arrive, each one confident of being his heir, only to be sent scornfully away by Mosca. Eager to gloat over his victims, Volpone sends Mosca (dressed as a gentleman) out into the streets to torment them, while he himself (disguised as a court-messenger) will go out to watch their annoyance. Meanwhile, Peregrine decides to torment Sir Politic, terrifying him with a report that the Venetian government is about to arrest him as an enemy of the state; the poor knight takes refuge in a tortoise-shell, to the amusement of Peregrine and his companions. Mosca now sees that his master has given him the opportunity he has been waiting for: he prepares a 'fox-trap'. But Voltore, Corvino and Corbaccio are furious at the way he has tricked them. When the court re-assembles to pass sentence on Bonario and Celia, Voltore confesses his earlier lies and places the blame on Mosca. Volpone now scents his danger and (still in his disguise) whispers to Voltore that Volpone is still alive and still means to make him his heir. Accordingly Voltore pretends to have a fit, thus suggesting that his confession was unreliable, and when he recovers he tells the now thoroughly confused judges that the rumour of Volpone's death is false. But at this point Mosca arrives in his gentleman's clothes and confirms that the rumour is true. Volpone at first tries to bargain with Mosca but finally throws off his disguise and reveals the real truth of the whole situation to the judges, who end the play by passing heavy sentences on all the guilty persons.

Detailed summaries

Dedication and Epistle

Written in dignified and difficult prose, this is Jonson's finest defence
of poetry and his own poetic values. He dedicates his play to the universities in recognition of the good judgement they showed in applauding it. Poetry should not be condemned because some poets are bad. It
·is a divine skill, an instrument for educating society. A good poet must
first be a good man. Though the theatre has a bad reputation, Jonson's
own plays do not deserve it. His satire, though sharp, has been directed
at vices, never at individuals or social groups. His aim is to reform the
stage; to set a good example by restoring the virtues of classical drama.
If the ending of his play seems too harsh for comedy, it proves that even
comedy can show justice being done, thus teaching men how to live well.
He promises to 'raise the despised head of poetry again . . . and render
her worthy to be embraced and kissed of all the great and master spirits
of our world.'

Prologue

Spoken by an actor who mediates between the author and the audience,
introducing the play. The use of a stumbling metre suggests that it may
have been spoken by Nano, the dwarf. Though the style is informal,
the content is serious. The author aims 'to mix profit with your pleasure.'
He has written fast, but instead of stringing together funny scenes to
amuse the crowd he 'makes jests to fit his fable' (that is, they are a
functional part of his plot). By 'quick comedy, refined / As best critics
have designed' Jonson means that his play is lively ('quick') while at the
same time following the rules of Aristotle and later theorists. On lines
31–32 see below (p. 45).

Act I Scene i

Volpone starts his day with a hymn in praise of gold which he describes
as 'the best of things' (line 16). But he tells Mosca that his chief pleasure
lies, not in *being* rich, but in clever methods of *becoming* rich. He despises
ordinary methods—trade, agriculture, industry, investment, money-
lending (lines 30–39)—and in a soliloquy reveals to the audience his
scheme for extracting gifts from 'clients' who hope to be made his heir;
he makes promises to each one separately and then makes them com-
pete against each other (lines 73–90).

COMMENTARY: We have already tried to visualise the opening (p. 11). Praising his gold (lines 3–27), Volpone looks like a priest engaged in religious ritual. His language, too, suggests Roman Catholic saint-worship: 'shrine' and 'saint' (line 2), 'adoration' and 'relic' (line 12). The imagery of this important speech is discussed on pp. 53–54; see also the analysis of this scene on pp. 62–63. Clearly the audience would be shocked by Volpone's blasphemy. In what ways would it also find him attractive? Consider the tone of the speech: joyful, positive, self-confident.

Look closely at Mosca in this scene; his flattery of his master is insincere, ironic. He says that Volpone's 'sweet nature' (line 48) stops him from lending money to 'fathers of poor families' and imprisoning them when they can't pay. What he really means is that Volpone avoids such people because they have nothing to offer him. Similarly Mosca pretends that Volpone would pity 'the widow's, or the orphan's tears' (line 49), but he means that Volpone would find these a nuisance. Note how Mosca manipulates his master into giving him a present. You are not a miser, he says (lines 52–61); you know how to use your wealth; you are not afraid to be generous (lines 62–3). Does Volpone perceive Mosca's insincerity? If not, this shows us from the start that Mosca is the cleverer of the two. But perhaps Volpone does perceive Mosca's game and is content to play along with him?

NOTES AND GLOSSARY

Ram:	the constellation Aries, which the sun enters in spring
Sol:	(*Latin*, sun), father of gold in alchemical theory
to boot:	in addition
purchase of:	method of obtaining
cocker up:	encourage

Act I Scene ii

Mosca presents Volpone with an entertainment acted by Nano (Italian 'dwarf'), Androgyno (Greek 'man-woman' or hermaphrodite) and Castrone (Italian 'eunuch'). The first part of this is a dialogue between Nano and Androgyno describing the transmigration of the soul of the Greek philosopher Pythagoras (6th century BC): after taking various shapes the philosopher's soul has finally entered the body of a fool (Androgyno). Secondly, Nano and Castrone sing a song in praise of fools. The show is interrupted when Voltore, the lawyer, is heard knocking. He has brought a large gold plate with Volpone's coat-of-arms engraved on it. Laughing to think of the lawyer's high hopes,

Mosca dresses Volpone in furs and night-caps and smears his face with ointment to make him look like a dying man.

COMMENTARY: The entertainment becomes easier to understand if the following points are noted:

(a) The verse is deliberately bad, indicating the poor literary taste of the 'author' (Mosca) and the 'audience' (Volpone). Mosca's bad taste is further shown by his having vulgarised two works of wit which Jonson admired: the dialogue is derived from Lucian's *The Cock* and the song from the ironic *Praise of Folly* by the Dutch humanist scholar Erasmus (1466–1536).

(b) The themes are appropriate to the play in ways that Mosca and Volpone don't recognise. Pythagoras' idea about the transmigration of souls—that the soul, after death, enters the body of another creature— is illustrated here in a way that emphasises Jonson's theme of human degeneracy. Similarly the theme of folly may serve to remind us that most of the characters in Jonson's play are 'fools' in the sense that they risk their souls by pursuing worldly aims.

(c) The scene is visually shocking and unpleasant. The three 'actors' are physically abnormal. The audience is meant to see their deformed bodies as a symbol of the spiritual deformity and abnormal values of Volpone. (This point is strengthened at I.v.43–47 when we are told that these creatures are Volpone's bastard children). But would the audience also enjoy their performance? Remember that in Jonson's day people paid money to see 'monsters' such as these in fair-grounds. Jonson tempts his audience to show its own bad taste by enjoying this show as much as Volpone does.

When Voltore knocks, Volpone makes his first reference to the fable of the Fox and the Birds (see above, p. 7):

> *Now, now, my clients*
> *Begin their visitation! vulture, kite,*
> *Raven, and gor-crow, all my birds of prey,*
> *That think me turning carcass, now they come.*

But four lines later he refers to another fable, the Fox and the Crow. In this the crow, carrying a cheese in its mouth, escapes from the fox by flying up into a tree. The fox flatters the crow by praising its beautiful voice. When the crow opens its mouth to sing, it drops its cheese and is left 'gaping' (line 97). This fable is appropriate to the lawyer who is praised for his eloquence in the law-courts.

The discussion between Volpone and Mosca at the end of the scene is accompanied by frenzied activity as the two rogues prepare to receive their first victim. Their high spirits and humour are infectious to the audience, which watches Volpone being transformed before its eyes from a virile, handsome man into a bed-ridden invalid. The following scenes give Volpone opportunities for playing the role of a sick man in several different ways. Though the effect is very funny, we can (if we wish) see Volpone's pretended sickness as another symbol of his diseased nature.

NOTES AND GLOSSARY
For classical references in the 'Entertainment' see notes in your edition
sleights: tricks
moyle: mule, traditionally ridden by lawyers
phthisic: asthma

Act I Scene iii

Voltore enters and presents his plate to the 'dying' Volpone. Mosca pretends to be working for him, and assures him that Volpone has made a will in his favour that morning. When further knocking is heard, the lawyer leaves, as though he had been paying a business call. Volpone and Mosca prepare for Corbaccio's visit.

COMMENTARY: The reader should consider how Voltore should be made to appear in order to suggest his character as 'vulture'. The same consideration should be given to the fox and the fly and to the other two birds of prey. How can costume, make-up, facial expression and physical mannerisms be used to suggest the 'animal' nature of these characters and their roles in the animal fable?

Much of the humour of this and the two following scenes springs from dramatic irony (see below, pp. 56–58). The audience shares a secret with Volpone and Mosca at the expense of their clients, who mistakenly think that they are sharing a secret with Mosca at the expense of Volpone. Thus, when Volpone accepts the plate and tells Mosca to ask Voltore 'to come more often', the audience sees a meaning which Voltore must suppose was unintended.

As a lawyer, Voltore is a man of the world who at first is sceptical about his good fortune. But he soon believes what he wants to believe. When he asks why Volpone has made him his heir, he is forced to accept Mosca's explanation (lines 52–66) which *sounds* complimentary but is in fact a series of concealed insults to himself and the legal profession. Analyse the irony of this speech carefully. Note, for example, the concealed image of lawyers as serpents (who can turn with 'quick agility', 'make knots,' and have 'forked' tongues) and remember that in the Bible Satan took the form of a serpent when he caused the Fall of Man by deceiving Eve in paradise (*Genesis*, 3). 'Humility' (line 60) *sounds* like a Christian virtue but its Latin derivation suggests 'creeping along the ground' like a snake. 'A suffering spirit' (line 62) *seems* to refer to the Christian virtue of patience (which means 'suffering'), but Mosca's real meaning is 'permissive'. Voltore is intelligent enough to see the insults in Mosca's speech, but he must pretend not to.

NOTES AND GLOSSARY

St Mark: the cathedral and square of St Mark, the centre of Venetian life, noted for goldsmiths' shops

chequeens: gold coins

Act I Scene iv

Corbaccio, old, blind and deaf, enters. He has brought Volpone a sleeping-draft, which Mosca wisely declines. (Throughout this visit Volpone pretends to be asleep, having supposedly suffered an apoplectic fit). The old man is pleased to hear the symptoms of Volpone's illness, which makes him feel younger and curious about the will. Mosca says that his master has not yet made his will. Suspicious of Voltore, whom he has seen leaving, Corbaccio produces a bag of gold coins to out-weigh Voltore's plate. But Mosca tells him that his best way of impress-ing Volpone is to make his own will in favour of Volpone instead of his son. Volpone will feel bound to reciprocate, so that Corbaccio, by sur-viving, can benefit his son twice over. The old man is delighted with this plan, which he claims to have thought of himself, and hurries off to prepare the new document. Volpone congratulates Mosca on his skill and moralises on the absurd delusions of old age. Then Corvino, the merchant, is heard knocking.

COMMENTARY: Though Volpone says almost nothing in this scene, remember that he can continue to show his reactions since Corbaccio has poor sight. He might, for example, show signs of excitement when Corbaccio produces his bag of gold coins.

As well as being funny, Corbaccio's mis-hearing of Mosca is used to reveal his nasty nature. (Find examples of this). Jonson stops us from feeling sorry for this very old man. Being near death himself, he is the greediest and most impatient of Volpone's clients. He is a murderer, since the 'opiate' he has brought (line 13) is presumably poisoned, though he would not wish it to be given to Volpone until he was sure that a will had been made in his favour. His meanness is shown when he sees an opportunity to take back his bag of gold (lines 80–81); when he refuses to give credit to Mosca for his plan (lines 109–111); and when he ignores Mosca's hinted request for a tip (lines 119–124). His eagerness to know the details of another person's illness is characteristic of old people: the worse Volpone is, the younger and stronger he feels. This blinds him to the obvious danger in Mosca's plan, that he (Corbaccio) will be the first to die.

Notice how Volpone's speech at the end of the scene (lines 144–159) expresses a 'true' point of view on the folly of wishing for long life. Though Jonson is always critical of Volpone and Mosca, he often speaks through them in criticising other characters.

NOTES AND GLOSSARY

brook:	endure
wont:	accustomed
elixir:	liquor sought by alchemists which gives eternal life
aurum . . .potabile:	touchable if not drinkable gold
take my venture:	take back my investment
gull:	cheat
battens:	grows fat

Act I Scene v

Corvino arrives, offering a pearl and a diamond. In this interview Volpone is awake and able to speak faintly, but is said to have lost his sight and hearing. So Mosca, having told Corvino that he is the heir, encourages him to overcome his scruples and shout abuse into Volpone's ear. After he goes, the two rogues are joyfully counting their 'good morning's purchase' when Lady Would-Be's visit is announced. But Volpone sends word that she should come back three hours later when he is 'high with mirth and wine'. The idea that her husband allows his wife to pay visits alone prompts Mosca to consider the different behaviour of Corvino, whose beautiful wife is kept shut up at home, guarded by spies. Volpone is interested and plans to visit her at her window—but in a different disguise.

COMMENTARY: Corvino appears unsure of himself in his first speeches and at lines 20–21 even shows pity for Volpone. We might think him 'better' than Voltore and Corbaccio, but this would be a mistake. Corvino is a man who is worse than he knows. His uncertainty how to behave ('How shall I do, then?') results from a basic lack of self-know-ledge, which he tries to conceal by behaving conventionally (as in "Las, good gentleman!'). We shall see that Corvino never loses this false image of himself as a good man. But his worry that Volpone can see what he is doing (lines 38, 50) reveals, not his conscience, but his fear of being found out. Mosca's task is to make Corvino display his true nature openly. This is done when, with obvious enjoyment, Corvino joins Mosca in shouting filthy abuse at Volpone (lines 61–66), and when he overcomes his scruples about murder (lines 70–74).

Mosca's last words to Corvino ('Your gallant wife, sir') carry a sinister emphasis which is explained when we discover that he has just found out about the existence of Celia. But meantime Jonson introduces Lady Would-Be to our notice. It is significant that on both occasions when she visits Volpone she arrives when she is not welcome. This makes her seem like a ridiculous nuisance, different from Volpone's other clients; like her husband, she is out of place in Venetian society. Mosca's remark 'She hath not yet the face, to be dishonest' (line 105) at first seems to mean 'She is not bold enough to misbehave,' but later events will show that he really means 'She is not pretty enough to be seduced.' This second meaning of 'face' leads Mosca to whet his master's interest in Celia's. The imagery of his famous speech beginning at line 107 will be discussed later (p. 55). Notice now, however, that Mosca links Celia's sex-appeal with the appeal of gold ('Bright as your gold! and lovely as your gold!'). And when he adds 'She's kept as warily as is your gold' he shows insight into his master's character. Mosca knows that, just as Volpone enjoys the 'cunning purchase' of his wealth 'more than the glad possession' (I.i.31–2), so also he will enjoy the challenge of seducing a woman who is hard to get.

NOTES AND GLOSSARY
visor:	mask
culverin:	type of gun
very draught:	veritable sewage-pit
to take my pearl:	by taking back my pearl

Act II Scene i

Outside Corvino's house. Sir Politic Would-Be seeks news from Peregrine who has recently arrived from England.

COMMENTARY: Sir Politic introduces himself by posing as a 'wise man', a citizen of the world, but he at once shows his folly by ridiculing

Ulysses, whom the Renaissance admired as the classical example of how wisdom could be acquired through travel. He looks even more foolish when he confesses that he has come to Venice in obedience to a whim ('humour') of his wife. The significance of his name is indicated when he refers to his 'dearest plots' (line 8)—the word 'politic' was associated in Jonson's time with the schemes or plots of a Machiavellian villain (see above, p. 10). Thus Sir Pol is not a 'would-be politician' in the modern sense of the phrase but is rather an amateur student of political intrigues (lines 100–105), and in Act IV he will recount his own schemes to benefit the state of Venice. The hopelessly unpractical nature of these schemes, and his ignorance of the real world around him, contrast with the effective plots and pragmatic realism of Volpone and Mosca. In this scene we see his superstitious interest in 'portents' (the raven, the lion, the porpoises and the whale) which had recently been observed in London when Jonson wrote. He also shows his absurdity by insisting that a well-known figure in London tavern-life, Stone the fool, had in fact been a Machiavellian secret agent.

NOTES AND GLOSSARY

laid for this height: aimed at this latitude
Spinola: Spanish commander in the Netherlands
porcpisces: (*Latin*, pig fishes) porpoises
your (line 74): see gloss on page 30
ordinary: eating-house
noddle: brain
ingenuous: noble

Act II Scene ii

Mosca and Nano enter and set up a platform on which Volpone (disguised as the mountebank Scoto of Mantua) delivers a dramatic speech to the crowd which has assembled to hear him. He claims that his magic oil, or ointment, can cure all diseases, and he offers a bonus to the first person who will buy it. Celia, appearing at her window, throws down money wrapped in her handkerchief, and Volpone offers her a powder which will preserve her beauty and keep her perpetually young.

COMMENTARY: Sir Pol (lines 9–13) is impressed by the false pretences of the Venetian mountebanks, but Peregrine (lines 14–19) expresses Jonson's own view of these notorious rogues (named from the Italian *monta in banco*, 'one who mounts on a bench'). Volpone gives a historically accurate demonstration of how they promoted worthless products by high-pressure sales-tactics, which often included song-and-dance entertainment. In this disguise Volpone is able to play an active, virile role for Celia's benefit, very different from the passive, invalid role which he plays for the benefit of his clients. Note how Celia, when we first see her dropping a handkerchief from her window, seems to be encouraging Volpone. The audience, which at this time knows her only from Mosca's description, is tricked into forming a false impression of her character.

NOTES AND GLOSSARY
quacksalvers: frauds
the state he keeps: his dignified behaviour
For historical and medical references in the mountebank's speech see notes in your edition

---

Act II Scene iii

Corvino enters and angrily drives the mountebank away. Sir Pol interprets the incident as part of a political plot and departs, followed by Peregrine who is amused by the Knight's stupidity.

COMMENTARY: 'Flaminio', 'Franciscina', 'Pantalone' are references to the Italian type of drama known as *commedia dell' arte* (see the notes in your edition on these names and those in the previous scene). By showing Sir Pol's fear of plots against himself, Jonson is preparing us for the trick to be played on him by Peregrine in Act V.

Act II Scene iv

Back home, Volpone complains that his longing for Celia is more painful than the blows he received from Corvino, and Mosca promises to find a way to satisfy his desires.

COMMENTARY: On the imagery of Volpone's speech about Cupid see below, p. 55. In the course of this scene Volpone's emphasis changes from his lust for Celia to his vanity in having given a successful performance as the mountebank. Which emotion do you think is stronger? And what significance do you find in Mosca's remark 'I have not time to flatter you' (line 37)?

NOTES AND GLOSSARY
horn him: make him a cuckold by seducing his wife; cuckolds (deceived husbands) were supposed to grow horns

Act II Scene v

Inside his house, Corvino criticises his wife for having encouraged the mountebank, and threatens to lock her up even more strictly than before. Then Mosca's arrival is announced.

COMMENTARY: In Corvino's angry speeches to Celia the audience would recognise the typical behaviour of a jealous Italian husband, obsessed with 'honour' (line 1) and threatening to take vengeance for his wife's infidelity on her entire family (lines 27–29). But the pleasure he takes in imagining Celia's lust may also suggest some sexual abnormality in himself, thus making his later treatment of her more believable. His reference to her as 'Lady Vanity' (line 21) is an 'English' touch in an Italian setting, alluding to a type of character in the morality plays exactly opposite to the type which the virtuous Celia really resembles (see above, p. 8).

NOTES AND GLOSSARY
dole of faces: range of expressions
fricace, for the mother: massage as treatment for hysteria (with secondary sexual meaning)
cittern: guitar

Act II Scene vi

Mosca brings news that his master's health has improved. He tells Corvino that Corbaccio and Voltore have restored him with Scoto's oil, and that they have hired doctors, at enormous expense, who are now recommending that the best cure for Volpone will be a young woman 'lusty, and full of juice, to sleep by him'. Mosca describes how Volpone's clients are competing with each other to provide this remedy—one of the doctors has offered his daughter—and he waits until Corvino makes up his mind to offer his wife. But he insists that Corvino should not bring Celia to Volpone's house until he is sent for.

COMMENTARY: Mosca's manipulation of Corvino is brilliant. He is too clever to tell his victim directly what to do. Instead, he plants the seed of an idea in Corvino's mind and allows it to grow until Corvino claims credit for having thought of it himself. Analyse the stages in this process between lines 46 and 95. Mosca puts Corvino into panic by stressing the need for a quick decision, rouses his jealousy against the rival doctor, assures him that the invalid is impotent, promises secrecy, and points out how easy it will be to murder Volpone in his next fit. Thus, as in their earlier scene together, Mosca does not need to corrupt Corvino: all he needs to do is to release the vicious instincts which Corvino already has, and which he does not recognise—he still sees himself as a man of 'honour' (line 72) and 'conscience' (line 90).

NOTES AND GLOSSARY
quean: young woman
Lupo: (*Italian*) wolf

Act II Scene vii

After Mosca goes, Corvino calls Celia and assures her that his earlier words had only been meant to test her. As proof of his confidence in her, he will take her to a feast 'where it shall appear / How far I am free, from jealousy, or fear.'

NOTES AND GLOSSARY
do (line 9):   do the act of sex

Act III Scene i

Mosca, on his way home, soliloquises on the art of the 'true' parasite.

COMMENTARY: Since he has just persuaded a jealous husband to prostitute his wife, Mosca is naturally pleased with himself. His talents are flourishing (lines 2–3); his blood tingles with the excitement of success (lines 3–5); he feels so light and active that he could 'skip' out of his body, as a snake sheds his skin. Glorifying his art, he turns normal values upside down much as Volpone had done in the opening speech of Act I. He praises the parasite's profession as divine in origin, and thinks his craft ('mystery') should be studied academically as a branch of learning. 'Liberally professed' has the double meaning of a profession suited to a gentleman and a profession that is widespread. Mosca's vision of human society as consisting entirely of parasites and sub-parasites, feeding off each other like animals, cynically reverses the ideal view of society as a hierarchy in which all ranks—masters and servants—work together for the common good. But Mosca is scornful of the ordinary type of parasite who flatters for the sake of a good meal or a place at court (lines 13–22). His ideal is the 'fine, elegant rascal' who can hit his target before anyone sees what he is aiming at, who can change direction and be everywhere at once, who can adapt himself to take advantage of every man's mood ('humour'), switching from one false face ('visor') to another with the speed of thought. This, Mosca says, is the 'true' parasite, whose genius is a gift of nature. We see that Mosca's delight in his skill seems, like Volpone's, to be almost an end in itself.

Act III Scene ii

Bonario, Corbaccio's son, passes Mosca in the street and refuses to speak to him because of his bad reputation. But Mosca tearfully protests his innocence and easily deceives the soft-hearted young man. Amazed to learn that his father is about to disinherit him as a bastard, Bonario agrees to go along with Mosca to hear proof.

COMMENTARY: Why does Mosca involve Bonario in his plot? We may guess that he means to kill Corbaccio, after the old man has willed his money to Volpone, and then to accuse Bonario of the murder. But this is uncertain. Jonson's main point is that Mosca's over-confidence ('Success hath made me wanton') here leads him into the first of the two mistakes which he makes in the play. He is so expert in manipulating vicious characters that he underestimates the danger which may result from involving the naive and innocent Bonario.

Act III Scene iii

While waiting for Mosca to bring news of Celia, Volpone amuses himself with his grotesque 'family'. When Lady Would-Be's visit is announced, he fears she will destroy his appetite for Celia and dreads what he is going to suffer.

COMMENTARY: Volpone's last speech here shows that Jonson intends the scene with Lady Would-Be to provide a contrast with the later scene with Celia. In the first scene Volpone will be the passive invalid, comically trying to escape under the bed-clothes from the Englishwoman's verbal assault. Later he will show himself as virile and sinister, actively trying to seduce and rape Celia.

Act III Scene iv

Lady Would-Be first adjusts her dress and her hair and scolds her waiting-women; then, dismissing the women, she approaches Volpone's bed and proceeds to deafen him with her conversation.

COMMENTARY: Little need be said of this scene except that it is very funny in performance. The humour is entirely free of the sinister elements which affect our laughter in most other scenes, and for once Volpone is the victim, so that we find ourselves sympathising with him. In Lady Would-Be we recognise a caricature of the supposedly emancipated woman (Renaissance version), eager to discourse on dreams, cures, music, literature, philosophy and the great love-story of her life. For her medical and literary references see the notes in your edition.

Act III Scene v

Mosca returns and rescues his master by telling Lady Would-Be that he has seen her husband rowing in a gondola 'with the most cunning courtesan of Venice'. He tells Volpone that his longing for Celia will soon be fulfilled, but that Corbaccio is expected first.

COMMENTARY: Though the comedy of Lady Would-Be is different in tone, notice how Jonson links it to the main plot by making it seem like parody. In her absurd way the lady, too, is after Volpone's money: her gift of a knitted night-cap provides a ridiculous parallel to the expensive presents of the three major clients. And Mosca's rescue of Volpone farcically anticipates Bonario's rescue of Celia. Why does Jonson introduce the hilarious scene with Lady Would-Be *before* the more disturbing scene with Celia? Does the sight of Volpone suffering comically in the first scene undermine his threatening behaviour in the second? Perhaps Jonson does this to prevent us from taking the rape-scene too seriously. Perhaps (more likely?) he is practising what modern dramatists call 'alienation', that is, forcing the audience to detach itself from the action and to *think* about its implications instead of responding emotionally.

NOTES AND GLOSSARY
bells ... pestilence: during outbreaks of plague, bells signalled the collection and burial of corpses
cock-pit: arena for cock-fighting (a noisy sport)
gamester: gambler
primero: a card-game

Act III Scene vi

Mosca has, of course, brought Bonario with him, so here he places him in hiding, supposing that the person knocking at the door is Corbaccio.

Act III Scene vii

It is not Corbaccio, however, but Corvino, who has brought Celia without waiting for Mosca's summons. So Mosca must tell Bonario that his father has been delayed and send him off to read in another part of the house. Meantime Celia is horrified to learn from her husband the reason for their visit. Corvino first tries persuasion, then threats, to force her towards Volpone's bed. Finally, at Mosca's suggestion, they leave her alone with Volpone. As she prays to 'God, and his good angels,' he leaps from his bed and begins to woo her ardently, offering her jewels, promising exotic food and drink and variety of love-making. Celia appeals to his better nature, his 'manliness,' but Volpone sees this as a challenge to his virility, and is on the point of raping her when Bonario leaps in and leads Celia away, vowing to bring Volpone to justice.

COMMENTARY: Occurring near the mid-point of the play, the scene is also central in Jonson's imaginative design. Celia's ordeal appears symbolic of the struggle of goodness to withstand the force of evil, as we see how her virtue is prostituted by her husband's greed to the animal lust of Volpone. It is Celia who expresses Jonson's clearest moral comments on the corrupt world of the play. She shows how, to her husband, 'heaven' and 'saints' mean 'nothing' (line 53), and how material values have deprived him of all sense of 'shame', 'honour' and 'modesty' (lines 133-8). To Volpone's offer of sensual delights she replies that the only wealth and pleasure she values is her innocence (lines 206-10); and she is even forced to condemn her own beauty as a 'crime of nature' because it seduces man's 'blood' (his passions) to rebel against the rule of moral judgement (lines 251-4).

But as well as being morally symbolic, the scene is intensely dramatic. Celia's sufferings are painful to watch, and Corvino repels us more than ever, first by his arguments—for instance, that by going to bed with Volpone Celia will be 'piously' ministering to the sick as well as helping her husband's career (lines 64-6)—and later by his violent and desperate threats (lines 96-106). While this struggle is going on, however, we are made to laugh with Volpone as he talks aside to Mosca (lines 68-9) and acts the role of the impotent old man (lines 81-9). It is typical of Jonson's method in *Volpone* that he forces us to laugh and to feel moral outrage *at the same time*. We experience a similar conflict of reactions in the second half of the scene when Volpone leaps from his bed and attempts to seduce Celia. Morally, of course, we condemn Volpone, not only for his lust but also for his vanity (lines 157-164), and because his

idea of the 'true heaven of love' (line 140) turns out to be a drunken orgy
in which he and Celia will 'act' sexual roles in a variety of disguises (lines
217–35). Yet at the same time we are likely to enjoy his splendidly confident performance. Disgusted by Corvino, we may be tempted to agree
with Volpone when he tells Celia, 'Thou hast in place of a base husband,
found / A worthy lover' (lines 186–7). Remember, too, that in the
theatre we can *see* the rich jewels and *hear* the splendid poetry with
which he tempts her:

> See, behold,
> What thou art queen of; not in expectation,
> As I feed others; but possessed, and crowned.
> See, here, a rope of pearl . . .
> See, a carbuncle . . .
> A diament, would have bought Lollia Paulina,
> When she came in, like star-light, hid with jewels,
> That were the spoils of provinces.

Though we notice that Volpone soon begins to talk nonsense—who
wants to eat 'the heads of parrots' or 'the brains of peacocks'?—we
must recognise that a Renaissance audience would have been excited
and attracted by Volpone as well as being shocked by his sinfulness.

Volpone's song (lines 165–83 and 236–9) is based on a famous poem
by Catullus (87–?47 BC), and at line 221 he refers to the *Metamorphoses*
of Ovid (43 BC–AD 18). Jonson admired these Roman poets as artists,
but by showing that Volpone admires them he criticises their sensuality.

Bonario's reference to Volpone's treasure as 'this dross, thy idol'
and to his treasure-chest as 'this altar' (line 272) carries our minds back
to the first scene where Volpone worshipped his gold as a god. This is
one of many ways in which Jonson reminds us that sexual immorality
(the subject of this scene) is closely linked to materialism.

NOTES AND GLOSSARY
On Volpone's classical allusions (lines 153–262) see notes in your edition

horn-mad:	obsessed about being cuckolded
the train:	the trap you have lured me into
fame:	reputation
jig:	joke
rotchet:	a fish
aquafortis, corsives:	acids
cope-man:	buyer
serene:	harmful mist

make up the antic: complete the grotesque dance
sounds man: shows your manhood (Volpone and the audience see a sexual meaning not intended by Celia)

Act III Scene viii

Mosca, whom Bonario has wounded on his way out, comes in to find Volpone in despair. He repents his error, and suggests they commit suicide 'like Romans', but a knock at the door soon revives his wit.

NOTES AND GLOSSARY
Saffi: Venetian policeman

Act III Scene ix

Corbaccio enters, followed at a distance by Voltore. Mosca turns the old man against his son by asserting that Bonario had threatened to kill both him and Volpone on account of the changed will. Voltore, over-hearing talk of a will, suspects Mosca of playing a double game, but Mosca persuades him that this plot is for his benefit, so that he can inherit Corbaccio's fortune as well as Volpone's. Mosca repeats to Voltore his tale of Bonario's violence, adding that Celia, who happened to be visiting the sick man, has been seized by Bonario and will be forced to give evidence that Volpone had tried to rape her. Seeing his hopes threatened, Voltore takes command and arranges that Mosca, Corbaccio and Corvino should meet with him at the Scrutineo (the law-court of the Senate). So Mosca, by his quick thinking, has already begun to organise a counter-attack to Bonario's accusation.

Act IV Scene i

Sir Pol lectures Peregrine on 'politic' behaviour; tells him of 'projects' which he hopes to sell to the Venetians; and allows him to read extracts from his diary.

COMMENTARY: The leisurely humour of this scene, and the absurd humour of the two scenes which follow, provide the audience with much-needed relaxation after the tense drama at the end of Act III. But the idiotic behaviour of the English characters continues to parody the more intelligent plotting and counter-plotting in the main action. Sir Pol and his wife show that they 'would be' like the Italians if only they *could* be. When we say that these scenes provide 'comic relief', we should notice that they don't give much comfort to an English audience. Jonson suggests that the English are no better than the Italians—just stupider.

NOTES AND GLOSSARY

your:	Sir Pol often uses 'your' when generalising, with no direct reference to the person addressed. (This idiom survives in some English circles today). Peregrine pretends to misunderstand him at line 9
garb:	behaviour
preposterous:	out of order
chandler:	candle-maker
hoy:	trading vessel
defalk:	reduce the price
arsenale:	the Venetian dockyards
cheapened:	bargained for

Act IV Scene ii

Lady Would-Be arrives and amazes her husband and Peregrine by insisting that the latter is the 'courtesan' in disguise. Sir Pol finally fears she may be right and departs in alarm. Peregrine, confused and angry, begins to suspect that Sir Pol has been trying to bring him and Lady Would-Be together.

NOTES AND GLOSSARY

The Courtier:	the best-known guide-book to courtly behaviour, by Baldassare Castiglione (1478–1529)
solecism:	a wrong use of words (the word itself is wrongly used here)
disple:	discipline
queen-apple:	a red variety

Act IV Scene iii

Mosca interrupts their quarrel and corrects the lady's mistake, offering to show her the real courtesan at the law-court. Lady Would-Be apologises to Peregrine and offers him hospitality, but her ambiguous language—'Pray you, sir, use me. In faith / The more you see me, the more I shall conceive'—confirms his suspicion that Sir Pol has been a 'bawd' to his wife, and he decides to take revenge in a 'counter-plot'.

COMMENTARY: Peregrine's suspicion that Sir Pol has prostituted his wife suggests another parallel with the main action. The fact that he is mistaken shows that even the least stupid of the three English characters is not quite as smart as he thinks.

NOTES AND GLOSSARY
callet: disreputable woman
salt-head: experience ('salt' is opposed to 'fresh')

Act IV Scene iv

At the law-court, Voltore has briefed Corvino and Corbaccio on the parts they will have to play. Mosca moves between the three men, assuring each one separately that the other two are being duped. He tells Voltore of another witness (Lady Would-Be) whom he can produce if necessary.

COMMENTARY: The rest of Act IV takes place in the law-court. Trials are themselves a form of drama, with conflict and suspense leading up to a verdict, and dramatists are fond of presenting them on stage. Here we see the lawyer in his own court behaving very confidently, but it is of course Mosca who controls the situation. His triumph is to have persuaded three characters, who (as we see here) deeply mistrust each other, to co-operate in a 'lie' (line 3) which will ultimately benefit none of them.

NOTES AND GLOSSARY
Mercury . . . French Hercules: both patrons of eloquence

Act IV Scene v

The four judges ('avocatori') enter, bringing with them Bonario and Celia, whose charges against Volpone they have already heard. The defendant is said to be too sick to come to court, but at Bonario's request he is summoned. Meantime Voltore presents the defence's case, which is based on the story invented by Mosca in III.ix but now also involves a slander on Celia: the court is told that her adulterous relationship with Bonario has been known for long and pardoned by Corvino, and is the reason why Corbaccio disinherited his son. As supporting witnesses Voltore produces first Corbaccio, who denounces Bonario and disclaims him as his son, and then Corvino, who calls his wife a whore. Celia faints. Mosca adds the evidence of the wound he received

from Bonario, and offers further evidence against Celia in the person
of Lady Would-Be.

COMMENTARY: The entry of the judges in their robes is visually impres-
sive. The court-scenes (which make up almost half of the remainder
of the play) are conducted with ceremonial dignity. The judges are
repeatedly called 'fathers'—as the senators in ancient Rome were
called *patres*—and in this way Jonson stresses that they ought to sym-
bolise authority and wisdom as well as justice and the rule of law.
Though we shall soon see that they are open to criticism, their first comments as they enter show that they have formed an accurate view of the
case after listening to Bonario and Celia.

Voltore gives a fine court-room performance, but his speech illus-
trates the corruption of rhetoric, using tricks of language to argue a
case which he knows to be false. Corbaccio, though he is too deaf to
follow the proceedings, manages to show his true nature by spitting
out words of abuse at his son. And Corvino, as we would expect, enjoys
reviling Celia—indeed his language is so foul that he has to be stopped
by the court (lines 119-20). He then asks to be reassured by Mosca that
there is no harm in what he is doing. We begin to see that the court is
fallible when the 4th Avocatore doubts the genuineness of Celia's faint.

NOTES AND GLOSSARY
stale . . . practice: decoy in his deceitful plot
laid: well-planned

Act IV Scene vi

Lady Would-Be enters and identifies Celia as the woman she claims to
have seen seducing her husband. The defence has now produced four
witnesses; Celia and Bonario, however, can only appeal to their 'con-
sciences' and 'heaven, that never fails the innocent' (lines 16-17). When
Volpone is carried in, Voltore clinches his case by asking if such a helpless invalid could commit rape. The judges order Bonario and Celia to
prison, send Volpone home 'with care', and retire, undertaking to pro-
nounce sentence later in the day. Mosca congratulates Voltore and re-
assures each of the clients separately, even promising Lady Would-Be
that he will persuade Volpone, in gratitude for her evidence, to name
her first in his will.

COMMENTARY: This is the first scene in which Lady Would-Be is made
to contribute to the main action of the play, and it shows us that the
Englishwoman is as greedy and unprincipled as the Venetians. The

court's exaggerated chivalry toward her becomes the turning-point in our respect for its judgement. After her evidence, the judges are sure that Bonario and Celia are guilty. Volpone's performance, though not really necessary, confirms the triumph of Mosca's scheme.

We have seen innocence abused and justice perverted. These are serious matters, but Jonson continues to let us laugh at Lady Would-Be and Volpone and to admire Mosca's skill.

NOTES AND GLOSSARY
affect venery: attempt love-making

Act V Scene i

Volpone, back home, describes the discomfort he has felt in the court-room and takes a drink to revive his spirits.

COMMENTARY: The last act opens with Volpone showing symptoms of fear: he has guessed, for the first time, what real sickness would be like. But he cannot face this reality. Wine soon restores his self-confidence, but it also makes him rash and so contributes to the mistakes which will cause his downfall.

Act V Scene ii

Mosca and Volpone celebrate their success, and Mosca tempts his master to play a further trick on their victims. Volpone sends Nano and Castrone to spread news that he has died, so that the 'birds of prey' and the 'she-wolf' will come for their reward. Mosca is named as the heir on a blank copy of the will. He is to put on a gentleman's gown and take an inventory of his new possessions, while Volpone is to stand behind a curtain and peep over to watch the disappointment of his clients.

COMMENTARY: Notice how Mosca subtly manipulates Volpone in this scene. When he says, 'this is our masterpiece: / We cannot think, to go beyond this' (lines 13–14), he knows that his master will want to go further. He encourages Volpone to 'cozen' Voltore (lines 42–7), and, although he pretends not to understand Volpone's plan (line 64), we guess that this is another example of how Mosca prefers to let his victims have the credit for ideas which suit his own purposes. His 'Yes' (line 75) may be spoken absent-mindedly, as though he is already considering how to use the opportunity of the will.

NOTES AND GLOSSARY
crump . . . louse: curl up like a wood-louse

Act V Scene iii

Voltore, Corbaccio, Corvino and Lady Would-Be arrive, one after the other, and struggle to read the will, while Mosca pretends to be busy with his inventory. Volpone watches with delight as they discover that Mosca is the heir, though Corbaccio's weak eyesight prevents him from getting the message until line 63, and Voltore remains convinced until line 80 that Mosca is really working for him. Scornfully lecturing each one in turn, Mosca sends them all home and blackmails them into silence by threatening to reveal their secrets. But Volpone wants to torment them still further. He sends Mosca (in the robe of a *clarissimo*) to pursue them in the street. He himself will do the same, disguised in the costume of a *commendatore* (a court messenger) which Mosca undertakes to procure.

COMMENTARY: Jonson provided only one stage-direction for this scene (*Volpone peeps from behind a traverse*, line 8). Though modern editors provide more, the scene is the best example in the play of how much can be left to the imagination by a good dramatic script. The four legacy-hunters enter separately, each one greeting Mosca eagerly. Then, while Mosca pretends to be too busy to notice them, and Volpone watches from over the curtain, they begin to circle slowly round the stage, glancing at each other suspiciously, like rival animals circling their prey. When Mosca casually throws the will over his shoulder—'There' (line 14)—they all pounce together and fight to get hold of it, like dogs over a bone.

The speeches with which Mosca sends each away should be studied carefully. He touches them at their weakest points, reminding them how well he knows them. Notice that at this point in the play the audience is made to identify with Mosca, accepting his right to make a moral judgement on the other characters.

Volpone is delighted with Mosca's performance, but Mosca enjoys playing the part of the heir more than Volpone realises. The latter's decision to carry the joke further is a rash mistake (see the comment on V.v. below).

NOTES AND GLOSSARY
Is his thread spun?: Is his life finished?
glazen-eyes: reference to Corbaccio's spectacles
wittol: a husband who knows he is being cuckolded
three legs: including his stick
costive: constipated

Act V Scene iv

Peregrine carries out the 'revenge' on Sir Politic Would-Be promised in IV.iii. Disguised as a merchant, he warns Sir Pol that Peregrine was a Venetian agent who has reported to his government that Sir Pol is plotting to sell Venice to the Turks, and that a warrant has been signed for his arrest. Sir Pol hides in a tortoise-shell which he has prepared for such an emergency. The merchants from whom Peregrine has obtained his disguise play the part of search-officers, and together with Peregrine they tease Sir Pol as he creeps around the stage. They pull off his shell and Peregrine reveals himself. After they leave, Sir Pol dreads the jokes that will be told of him. He hears that his wife has come home 'melancholic'. Both decide to leave Venice for ever.

COMMENTARY: Since Peregrine was mistaken in regarding Sir Pol as a bawd, his revenge may seem cruel and excessive. But *Volpone* is a play in which vice and folly are shown to be closely connected. Though Sir Pol is not clever enough to hurt anyone, he is the type of fool who 'would be' more harmful if he could, and therefore deserves some punishment. Clearly the ridiculous humiliation he suffers here is meant as a contrast to the harsher punishments later inflicted on the more serious offenders.

The tortoise, because it carries its house on its back, was regarded in the Renaissance as a symbol of 'home'. From Sir Pol's last words we can infer that Jonson used this symbol to suggest that foolish Englishmen should remain in their own country instead of advertising their folly overseas.

NOTES AND GLOSSARY

exact him: force him out
fugitive-punk: disguised prostitute
frail: type of basket
engine: device, contraption
motion: puppet-show
freight . . . gazetti: reported in the newspapers

Act V Scene v

After congratulating each other on their new costumes, Volpone sets out for the law-court and Mosca reveals to the audience that he means to blackmail his master and make him pay for his sport. He sets Volpone's 'family' free.

COMMENTARY: Volpone, for the sake of a laugh, has announced his own death and made Mosca his heir. Mosca's 'fox-trap' is to insist publicly that this is the truth, thus forcing Volpone to bargain with him. That the master has now surrendered power to his servant is emphasised (*a*) by the house-keys which Mosca holds and (*b*) by their clothes: Mosca is now dressed as a gentleman and Volpone as a mere messenger.

NOTES AND GLOSSARY
case: disguise

Act V Scene vi

As Corbaccio and Corvino prepare to return to the court-room, the 'messenger' enters and teasingly congratulates them on their good fortune in having inherited Volpone's wealth.

COMMENTARY: In this and the three following scenes the stage represents different parts of a street or square. The action is continuous. Volpone, after his first entrance, never leaves the stage, but the fact that the other characters enter and re-enter, crossing the stage at different angles, gives the audience the impression that the scene changes. (Note Volpone's reference to 'at the next corner,' V.vii.23).

The purpose of these scenes is (*a*) to emphasise the embarrassment of the disappointed clients; (*b*) to show Mosca enjoying his role as a *clarissimo*; (*c*) to show Volpone carried away recklessly by his delight in taunting his victims. Volpone's behaviour here may remind us of the *hubris* of Greek tragic heroes (the arrogance and insolence which often precedes their downfalls).

Act V Scene vii

Volpone similarly teases Voltore by offering to buy a brothel which he has supposedly inherited.

Act V Scene viii

The sight of Mosca in his robe angers Corbaccio and Corvino, and Volpone infuriates them even more by expressing surprise that they allowed themselves to be cheated by a parasite.

NOTES AND GLOSSARY
moral emblems: recalling the fable of the fox and the crow
basilisk: fabulous creature which kills by staring

Act V Scene ix

Mosca snubs Voltore, and Volpone says he cannot imagine how such a
learned man could be tricked.

NOTES AND GLOSSARY
biggin: lawyer's cap
familiar: member of his household
mule: compare I.ii.108

Act V Scene x

The court re-assembles at the Scrutineo, with Bonario and Celia,
Corbaccio and Corvino. Voltore enters, accompanied by Volpone
(still in his disguise). At once the lawyer creates a sensation by confes-
sing that his earlier story had been false and asking pardon from the
judges. He lays the blame on Mosca, and the court sends Volpone (as
'messenger') to fetch him. Corvino, in alarm, argues that Voltore has
gone mad, 'distracted' by disappointment. When the judges learn that
Volpone is dead and Mosca the heir, they fear they have treated Mosca
disrespectfully by sending their messenger to fetch him; they now send
the Notario (registrar) to invite him more politely. They do not know
if they should believe Voltore's confession.

COMMENTARY: Though all three clients are equally angry with Mosca,
Voltore is the only one who dares call Mosca's bluff and confess the
truth for the sake of revenge. As a lawyer he knows that the court may
pardon a criminal whose confession serves to bring a worse criminal
to justice.

Act V Scene xi

Volpone, on his way to fetch Mosca, regrets his own stupidity in having
provoked Voltore too far. When he meets his 'family', he suspects for
the first time that Mosca may be tricking him. He sends them to tell
Mosca to come to the court. He himself will return there to persuade
Voltore to change his story.

NOTES AND GLOSSARY
crotchets, conundrums: word-games for his amusement

Act V Scene xii

The judges have been studying Voltore's written statement of the case. What puzzles them is that Voltore's belief in Volpone's impotence cannot be reconciled with Celia's account of attempted rape. Volpone (still in his disguise) returns and informs the court that Mosca is coming. Then he whispers to Voltore a message from Mosca that the story of Volpone's death was intended as a test of his reactions and that he is still the heir. At Volpone's suggestion, the lawyer discredits his earlier confession by pretending to be mad (as Corvino had said he was). He falls down in a fit, and Volpone and Corvino claim to see the devil—the cause of his madness—leaving his body in the shape of a blue toad with bat's wings. When he 'recovers', he says that every word in his statement is false, and that Volpone is alive. At this moment of confusion Mosca arrives in his robe. The judges treat him with respect; one of them even marks him as a possible husband for his daughter. Volpone appeals to Mosca to say he is alive, but Mosca refuses to recognise him and tells the court he has come from ordering his patron's funeral. Volpone now sees Mosca's treachery. When Mosca under his breath demands half his wealth, Volpone at first refuses; then, when he accepts, Mosca demands more. Mosca claims to be irritated by this insolent 'messenger' and the court orders the messenger to be whipped.

Faced with the prospect of a whipping and of losing all he has, Volpone prefers to reveal himself. Rather than see Mosca use his wealth to marry into the aristocracy he decides to ruin Mosca as well as himself. He removes his disguise, identifies the other villains, and asks the court to pass sentence. The whole situation is now clear to the judges. Though Celia pleads for mercy, the first Avocatore ignores her plea and proceeds to judgement. Mosca, for his part in the plot and for posing as a gentleman, will be whipped and spend the rest of his life as a prisoner in the galleys. Volpone, being a gentleman, cannot receive the same sentence, but his wealth is to be given to a hospital and he is to be kept in prison until he is as sick as he has pretended to be. Voltore is dismissed from his profession and banished from Venice. Corbaccio is to hand over his estate to his son and retire to a monastery. Corvino is to be rowed round Venice wearing ass's ears and placed in the stocks, and he is to send Celia home to her father with her dowry trebled.

COMMENTARY: The first part of this final scene is confusing to read, but the action is logical and clear in performance. Volpone's success in making the lawyer retract his confession is important for two reasons. First, it shows that Voltore, who has seemed to be obeying his conscience, is easily persuaded to disregard it when his hopes of getting rich are revived. (It is ironically appropriate that the 'intelligent' lawyer is willing to pretend to be mad). Second, Volpone's counter-attack restores our respect for his skill after his earlier mistakes and maintains suspense until the end of the play. The possibility that justice will again be thwarted remains strong until the partnership of Volpone and Mosca is finally broken.

The second mistake which Mosca makes in the play is to suppose that his master will be content to escape by being 'dead'. For comment on the breakdown of their partnership see below, pp. 63–4. On the court's final judgements see pp. 66–7. On the Epilogue spoken by Volpone see p. 67.

NOTES AND GLOSSARY

proper: handsome
uncase: remove his disguise
chimera: fabulous animal, part-lion, part-goat, part-serpent; 'incredible mixture'
substance: property
berlino: pillory, wooden structure with holes enclosing the head and arms of the offender

Part 3

Commentary

When Shakespeare wrote a play, he usually began with a well-known story, or a story which had been told by another writer, and then let his imagination work on it until he had transformed it into something new. A result of this method is that readers of Shakespeare have to use their own imaginations in following his, and end by interpreting his plays in many different ways. Jonson's method was the opposite. He began with a clear idea of what he wanted to say, and then invented a story which would make his meaning clear. So, since there is not much doubt about his meaning in *Volpone*, we can start by identifying his themes—we have met most of them already—and then go on to examine the art with which he expressed them.

Themes and morals

The purpose of living

At the end of the play, when Volpone says 'we all can hope / Nought, but a sentence' (V.xii.92–3), his surface meaning is that he and the other criminals have nothing left to hope for except the judgement of the court. But his words also remind us that, for all human souls, the only thing worth living for is a favourable verdict at the Day of Judgement. To lead a Christian life, to live as God means us to live, is therefore good 'policy', because heaven is the only 'wealth', the only 'inheritance', which ultimately matters. This is the deepest, though not the most obvious, message of the play. This is what Jonson means by 'the best reason of living' which poetry should aim to teach (The Epistle, lines 107–8). It is the 'cause of life' which Celia laments that men like her husband have abandoned (III.vii.136).

Crime and folly

Since *Volpone* is a satire, it teaches that lesson indirectly. Most of the time it focuses on the crimes which human beings commit when they forget Christian teaching and follow their appetites. Crime, however, is seen as a kind of folly, since it is foolish to practise short-sighted policies for the sake of short-term, worldly rewards. And folly, correspondingly, is shown to be a kind of crime. Man has a duty to cultivate his reason to enable him to distinguish between right and wrong. If he neglects that duty, it becomes a matter of chance whether he commits crime (like Lady Would-Be) or fails to commit it (like Sir Pol). Stupidity is no excuse. This close connection between crime and folly is an important part of Jonson's satiric vision.

Disease and abnormality

Every man is responsible for his actions. When Volpone says 'to be a fool born, is a disease incurable' (II.ii.159), he seems to suggest that a man cannot help being a fool any more than he can help falling sick. But 'disease' and 'sickness', which are mentioned very often in the play, rarely have their usual meaning of accidental misfortunes. Jonson uses them as spiritual metaphors. Sickness is the state which man brings on himself by ignoring the Christian rules for spiritual health. Disease is a description of man's 'fallen' nature. Thus Volpone's pretence of being physically ill is an appropriate symbol of his spiritual state. Even when the physical ailments are real, as in Corbaccio, we continue to see them as symbolic. Corbaccio is spiritually deaf and blind, failing to realise that his end is near, and that he should be thinking about the state of his soul.

Abnormality is treated in a similar way. We might want to feel sorry for the dwarf, the eunuch and the hermaphrodite, but Jonson uses these creatures as symbols of the abnormal values of their father. Like disease, abnormality is presented not as a misfortune but as a moral fault. The normal way to live is the right way to live—the way God intends and teaches us to live. In this sense Volpone is immediately seen to be abnormal when he worships his gold instead of God and finds more satisfaction in wealth than in the love of 'children, parents, friends' (I.i.17).

Greed and pride

No one can miss that Volpone is a satire on greed. We are shown, not not just one or two individuals, but almost a whole society driven by the love of money. Even the judges treat Mosca with respect when they think he has become rich. Most of the play is a story of *competitive* greed. We first see the greed of Volpone and Mosca in competition with the greed of the clients. Increasingly we become aware of the clients competing against each other. And finally we see competition breaking out between Volpone and Mosca. All this is obviously a picture of how society behaves. *Volpone* has been studied as a comment on the rise of capitalism. In Jonson's day, in the same way as people were becoming interested in the Machiavellian science of how power actually operates (instead of thinking in theological terms of power as authority delegated by God through the social hierarchy), so also it was becoming clear that the individual who was able to make money could achieve more actual power than rulers who relied on authority alone and were often short of cash. Certainly *Volpone* was written in response to a social development which we now recognise as the beginning of the capitalist free-enterprise system. (On this see L.C. Knights, *Drama and Society in the Age of Jonson*). But the urge to get rich has never been a new phenomenon. Jonson was studying one of the oldest and most basic of human instincts, the greed for possessions. And he sees it as a disease. As the 1st Avocatore says at the end of the play: 'These possess wealth, as sick men possess fevers, / Which, trulier, may be said to possess them' (V.xii.101–2). We should remember, too, that wealth is not the only thing which Volpone is greedy for. At the centre of the play is his lust for Celia, his desire to possess another person. For every type of pleasure Volpone has an insatiable appetite.

According to the church, greed was the root of all evils (*radix malorum est cupiditas*), but it was not the worst of all sins. The chief of the Seven Deadly Sins was pride (*superbia*). This is the state of self-satisfaction, of forgetting our dependence on God, closely related to what we now call vanity. In Volpone and Mosca we see this emphasised even more than their greed. Their deepest motive is to satisfy their vanity, their pride in themselves and especially their skills. 'I glory,' says Volpone, 'More in the *cunning purchase* of my wealth, / Than in the glad possession' (I.i.30–32). He enjoys the triumph of their skill in the lawcourt 'more, than if I had enjoyed the wench: / The pleasure of all woman-kind's not like it' (V.ii.10–11). Mosca, too, continually finds satisfaction in his skill ('I . . . grow in love / With my dear self,' III.i.1–2), even when it brings him no material reward. And in the last scene of the play he seems more interested in being treated like a gentleman than in becoming rich, though of course the two things go together. Jonson explains the acquisitive instinct (our urge to possess things) as an outgrowth of the even more basic instinct of self-love (our need to form a flattering image of ourselves).

Disguise and role-playing

To flatter oneself is to seek to escape from one's real nature. As was mentioned in the Introduction, Jonson held the belief (Stoic as well as

Christian) that man must examine his real nature, attempt to improve it, and *then remain true to it*.

Polonius expresses this idea in Shakespeare's *Hamlet* when he gives advice to Laertes:

> *This above all, to thine own self be true,*
> *And it must follow, as the night the day,*
> *Thou canst not then be false to any man.*

Celia and Bonario are characters who are 'true' in this way to themselves and to others, constant and unchanging, but most of Jonson's characters are 'false' to each other because they do not face the truth about themselves. The 'self' Mosca says he is in love with is not really his self but his art, which consists in suppressing the self and adapting it to circumstances (III.ii.26–29). The clients never recognise the full extent of their wickedness, and Corvino, especially, always sees himself as a man of honour. We might suppose that Volpone is less guilty of hypocrisy, since he always knows what he is doing, but in fact he is continually running away from his self by acting roles, by pretending to be what he is not. ('Hypocrite' is the Greek word for 'actor'). Volpone plays the invalid in Acts I, III and IV, the mountebank in Act II, and the court-messenger in Act V. He even wants to make love in disguise (III.vii.221–33). When he removes his last disguise and proudly declares 'I am Volpone' (V.xii.89), we wonder if he really knows who Volpone is. Perhaps we should see his final gesture as the biggest act of all.

Comedy and laughter

So far this survey of themes has made *Volpone* sound like a severe sermon. But we know, if we have experienced it properly, that it is not a sermon but a highly dramatic and very funny play. How do we explain this contradiction? The answer is that one of Jonson's main concerns in this play—we can almost call it a theme—is the relationship between the theatre and morality.

The basis of drama is disguise and role-playing: actors escaping from themselves and pretending to be other people, doing (in fact) exactly what Jonson thought that human beings should not do. A good actor is one who, like Volpone, can play any number of roles and never be recognised; a bad actor is one who, like Celia, is always recognisably himself. Similarly, the characters who appeal to us most in drama are those who keep surprising us by changing, whereas those who never change at all are apt to be dull. This is to say that, in the theatre, we enjoy the opposite qualities to those which we admire, or should admire, in real life. The qualities which Jonson disapproves of in Volpone and Mosca—their ability to adapt themselves and play roles—are the same qualities which make these characters theatrically exciting. We can understand why Jonson, as a moralist, had a deep distrust of the dramatic medium. But it is also obvious that, as a dramatist, he enjoyed Volpone and Mosca and enjoyed his dramatic skill in creating them. Thus the conflict between moral values and theatrical values is part of the meaning of his play. He experienced the conflict himself and took care that his audience would experience it also.

At the heart of the conflict is the question of laughter. Audiences who pay to see a comedy expect a good laugh. But, when we relax and enjoy ourselves in the theatre, we often laugh thoughtlessly at things which would not seem funny in real life, things which we know we ought not to laugh at when we consider them more seriously. In particular, when we laugh *with* certain characters at the expense of others, we identify ourselves with the characters whose amusement we share. Throughout most of Jonson's play we laugh *with* Volpone and Mosca and in that way we show our tolerance, even our approval, of their values. Our laughter tends to compromise us morally. This is a subject we shall return to in the section on 'Rhetoric and irony'.

Structure

Structure influenced by themes

It is easy to see that *Volpone* was designed to emphasise the themes we have listed. To take the last idea first, Jonson's interest in the way our enjoyment of drama often conflicts with our standards of morality led him naturally to what is called 'rogue-comedy'—to tell the story of a rogue, in this case *two*, who are morally inexcusable but whom we cannot help admiring for their skill and enjoying for their humour and high spirits. Because he was fascinated by what the human mind could achieve when free from all moral restraint, Jonson needed a story which would give full scope to Mosca's cleverness in manipulating people and finding ways out of trouble. And in order to stress his idea that people play roles to escape from their selves, he had to build Volpone's part around a sequence of great 'performances'. We can see, too, how his view of Volpone's moral sickness led him to put special emphasis on the role of the invalid, so that Volpone's sick-bed becomes a focus for much of the action. Most obviously of all, Jonson's vision of society's competitive greed prompted him to use the fable of the fox and the birds, in which all the animals are equally selfish and greedy, though not equally intelligent. And since he saw money as the principal object of human greed, he made Volpone's wealth the centre of his structure, a magnet to attract the worst instincts in all his characters.

Classical principles of plot-structure

In constructing his play Jonson was not only intent on emphasising his themes; he was also concerned, as he tells us in his Prologue (line 30), to make a comedy 'as best critics have designed'. He cared about the theories of dramatic form which Renaissance scholars had developed from their study of Aristotle's *Poetics* and the Roman comedies of Terence. In all these theories the most important principle was *unity* : that every part of a play should contribute to a single, total effect. In particular, the Prologue (lines 20–28) shows Jonson's hostility to the common practice in English comedy of introducing comic scenes which, though funny in themselves, had no relevance to the plot. Jonson appreciated that there were 'laws' and 'rules' for the writing of good comedy, and he was willing to follow them when he saw they were 'needful':

> *The laws of time, place, persons he observeth,*
> *From no needful rule he swerveth.*

We shall consider the 'law of persons' in the section on 'Characters'. The laws of time and place were based on the belief that the plot of a play would be more believable, and its impact more forceful, if it described the events of a single day occurring in a single geographical location (usually a city). Shakespeare proved that these laws could be disregarded without serious damage to a play's unity, but *Volpone* is a good example of how effective they could be.

The action of *Volpone* begins in the morning and ends on the evening of the same day. It opens with Volpone getting out of bed ('Good morning to the day'), engaging in a morning act of worship to his gold, and watching a morning entertainment before starting the morning's business (receiving his clients). He puts off Lady Would-Be until 'some three hours hence' (I.v.98), and it is still morning when he performs as the mountebank under Celia's window (see III.vii.149). In the afternoon he receives Lady Would-Be, then Corvino and Celia. The court-scene in Act IV takes place later in the afternoon, and the judges promise to pass sentence on Bonario and Celia 'ere night' (IV.vi.61). Some readers find a fault in this time-scheme when Volpone tells Celia

(III.vii.148) that he has already visited her window several times in different disguises. They point out that he had never heard of Celia until that morning. But we should probably suppose that he is lying to Celia to persuade her that he has been in love with her for a long time. In general, the effect of compressing the action into a single day is *(a)* to convey the eagerness of Volpone and Mosca to make use of every moment of their lives ('Time will not be ours for ever'); *(b)* to increase the audience's sense of the pressure and excitement of the plot; and *(c)* to emphasise the dramatic reversals in the fortunes of characters who can be 'up' one moment and 'down' the next.

The 'law of place' did not mean that the scene could never change—in *Volpone* there are several street-scenes as well as scenes in Volpone's bedroom, Corvino's house and the law-court. Audiences in Jonson's day were quick to accept such changes. But the advantages of setting the whole play in a single city hardly need to be stressed. Jonson was able to concentrate his action and also establish the reality of what he meant by 'Venice'. A symbol of decadent materialism could be made persuasively real.

All Aristotle's followers agreed that the unity which mattered most was unity of action, and that the test of this was that no incident could be removed from the plot without destroying a pattern of logically-connected events. It may therefore seem surprising that Jonson introduced the story of the English travellers. Peregrine and Sir Politic Would-Be play no part in the main story and never appear on stage along with Volpone; they could be removed from the play quite easily. Though Lady Would-Be does join forces with the other legacy-hunters in IV.vi and V.iii, even she can hardly be called essential to the main plot's logical development. We have an example here of how Jonson could assert his independence from the rules when he needed to do so. As we have seen, he needed the Would-Bes to provide a link between Venice and England. By separating Sir Pol from Volpone he at first seems to emphasise the *difference* between absurd English folly and intelligent Italian vice. But by gradually associating Lady Would-Be with the Italians he ends by showing that the difference is less great than his audience might have wished to believe.

The movement of the play

The most practical questions which face a dramatist as he writes are questions of structure: questions of what to put in and what to leave out. Structure means 'building' a play so that its parts will fit firmly and easily together; it involves taking care that characters develop consistently, that their actions are properly motivated, that loose ends in the story are avoided. It is often said jokingly that Jonson, who had been trained as a bricklayer in youth, constructed his plays like buildings, laying brick after brick with the intention that his structure would stand firm for ever. The comparison is useful up to a point, but we need to remember that plays differ from buildings by being continually in motion. A dramatist chiefly shows his structural skill by controlling the movement of his play so that it will achieve the maximum impact on an audience.

Compared with later acts, Act I moves slowly, because its function is to make the audience familiar with the situation from which the later action will develop. Thus we are shown:

(a) Volpone himself and his 'religion'
(b) His household: Mosca and the 'family' and their sense of humour
(c) The essential relationship of Volpone and Mosca
(d) Their means of extracting gifts from their clients.

The three scenes with Voltore, Corbaccio and Corvino are closely parallel, and might have been monotonous but for Jonson's skill in varying them subtly. In the first scene the dying man can speak, in the second he is speechless, in the third he is totally deaf. Near the end of the act, when Mosca mentions Corvino's wife and arouses Volpone's interest in her, we are alerted to the direction which the plot is about to take.

Act II opens by introducing more characters, Sir Pol and Peregrine. Here *variety* of humour and *contrast* with the characters of Act I are Jonson's main concern. When we next see Volpone it is clear that the action is beginning: the pace of the play begins to quicken as Volpone changes from a passive invalid into a super-dynamic salesman. The blows he receives from Corvino mark the first slight check to his growing self-confidence, but the setback is momentary and recovery is achieved when Mosca persuades Corvino to make a gift of his wife.

The pattern of success-reverse-recovery forms the main movement of the play, as Volpone's fortunes alternately rise and fall. (Mosca's fortunes coincide with Volpone's until half-way through Act V). At the start of Act III they have reached their first peak of achievement: whatever they do seems bound to succeed, and we enjoy their success, though we are beginning to feel worried about what will happen to Celia. But Act III will end with the first of their major disasters. Since this is caused by Mosca's mistake in bringing Bonario to Volpone's house, Mosca is made to open the act with a boastful soliloquy. A small-scale setback is the visit of Lady Would-Be when Volpone is expecting Celia. Since Volpone's lust for Celia is likely to turn the audience against him, Jonson cleverly arouses some sympathy for him by showing him first in the laughable situation of being 'raped' by Lady Would-Be. The scene with Celia is the centre of the play's structure. Earlier scenes have prepared for it, and most of the later scenes follow as a result. Symbolically, too, it is a climax in the struggle between evil and good. Bonario's intervention, exposing Volpone and wounding Mosca, suddenly reduces the two rogues to a state of despair where they contemplate suicide.

The movement of Act IV shows their recovery from despair to a peak of success even higher than before. Mosca achieves this by making his victims do most of the work. Whereas earlier he had dealt separately with each, his greater triumph now is to force them to co-operate to get Volpone acquitted. Mosca's triumph should also be seen as a triumph of plot-structure on the part of Jonson. He shows what sacrifices people will make for the sake of their overwhelming greed. A lawyer will dishonour his profession, an old man will disown his son, a husband will publicly proclaim himself a cuckold, a wife will confess that her husband has gone off with a prostitute. Evil had failed in Act III, but now it succeeds in persuading the court to send innocent characters to prison.

The structure of the last act is simple in outline. Evil destroys itself; Volpone and Mosca destroy each other. Again, over-confidence leads to disaster; each makes a fatal mistake in misjudging the other. Their triumphant laughter at the start of the act gives place to the grim tone of the court's final judgements. But Jonson complicates that simple pattern by introducing Voltore's court-room confession which Volpone persuades him to withdraw. It is typical of the structure of Jonson's comedies that he gives a new movement to his plot at the last moment, just when the audience is beginning to think that it sees the end coming. So, when Volpone has admitted his mistake and foresees disaster, Jonson makes him fight back and very nearly succeed. The second court-scene almost ends like the first. Our admiration for Volpone's boldness and skill is maintained until the play's final moments. Jonson challenges us to reconcile our admiration with the harsh justice of Volpone's punishment.

Characters

Jonson's method of characterisation

In the same way as Jonson made a plot to fit his themes, so also he made characters to fit his plot. Obviously, in any good play, the plot and the characters will depend on each other so closely that it is hardly worth asking which was more important to the author. But if we think of a play like *Hamlet*, we would probably agree that Shakespeare's interest in the personality of the central figure is stronger than his interest in the plot. It is because Shakespeare wants to explore Hamlet's mind that the action is delayed by his long soliloquies. Jonson, however, never thought of characters as portraits of unique individuals worth studying for their own sake. For him, a character in a play was a character in a play—a figure who contributes to a larger design. And one of the main requirements of the classical 'law of persons' which he followed was that every character should represent some typical human quality, or typical combination of qualities, so that the pattern of interaction between the characters would be typical of human society. In that way it was felt that the dramatist's imitation of life would be universally true, and that the moral he taught would be universally applicable.

Any good work of art persuades us to accept the conventions it follows. Nobody watching a performance of *Volpone* is likely to complain that the characters are 'unreal', though it is a fact that we would not meet such people in real life. Like most satirists, Jonson works through exaggeration, through caricature, but the effect of caricature is to remind us of reality very forcibly. Having decided what qualities he wishes to illustrate, he brings them vividly to life, and can penetrate deeply into human psychology.

Jonson's method does mean, however, that it is pointless to try to 'understand' his characters sympathetically, as though they were real people. Rather, we are required to judge what they stand for as part of our moral response to the play. But we cannot judge Jonson's characters, as we might judge Shakespeare's, by balancing good moral qualities against 'flaws', or bad moral qualities against 'redeeming features'. Morally, all the main characters in *Volpone* are either wholly bad or wholly good. Judging them becomes a difficult and fascinating exercise because Jonson continually and very deliberately tries to upset our moral standards.

This process can be summarised briefly. At one extreme, the three 'birds of prey' present no problem, since their evil is obvious and repellent, but it becomes one of the many factors in the play which confuse our judgement of Volpone and Mosca, making us think of them favourably by comparison. At the other extreme; Celia and Bonario are obviously good, but it is difficult to respond to their goodness with enthusiasm, and we must question whether their goodness is effective in overcoming evil. The Would-Bes have no moral virtue, but we are always being tempted to forgive their stupidity. The judges represent the authority of the state, but how far do they command our respect? The main test of our judgement is of course our response to Volpone and Mosca. Their moral wickedness is never in doubt, but it is quite impossible to condemn them coldly because, for other reasons, we enjoy and admire them so much.

Such tests of our moral responses are the basis of the play. Spectators or readers must experience them for themselves. Although this book points continually to the challenges which Jonson offers through his characters, it is not in the last resort possible to tell the reader how to react.

Additional notes on characters

The following is a selection of points about Jonson's characters which may be used to supplement points made in Part 2.

To begin with a practical question: how old is **Volpone?** Readers tend to exaggerate his age because he is often referred to as 'old' by characters who only know him in his disguise as a dying man (see II.vii.17; IV.v.81). In production he is usually shown in his mid-forties. Jonson seems to envisage his beard and eyebrows as red, fox-like (II.iv.30). His vanity about his personal appearance (III.vii.157–64) and about his virility (ibid.260–63) suggests that he is still very vigorous. Clearly his disguise as a sick man, with ointment smeared on his face, is not one which flatters him. He associates the invalid role with being 'dead' (I.iv.162) and comes to 'life' when he thinks about Celia: 'My blood, / My spirits are returned; I am alive' (III.v.34–35).

Because he lives for pleasure (I.i.70–72: I.v.86–89), he resents the discomfort he feels in the court-room (V.i.2–10). But he derives the greatest of all his pleasures from his acting-skill and from laughing at those who are deceived by his disguises. His need to laugh becomes obsessive in Act V. He longs for

Any device, now, of rare, ingenious knavery,
That would possess me with a violent laughter. (V.i.34–35)

Watching the disappointment of his clients gives him 'a rare meal of laughter' (V.ii.87). This appetite for laughter, or 'sport', causes his mistake of pursuing his victims into the street and leaving Mosca in charge. As Mosca says, he must pay for his sport (V.v.18). His own speeches on this subject (V.xi.1–5, 13–17) should be studied.

'Rare' is a favourite word for Volpone. We have just seen him apply it to 'knavery' and 'laughter'; he also asks about Celia, 'Hath she so rare a face?' (I.v.107). He admires rarity because he wants to be exceptional, different from ordinary men. 'I gain / No common way' (I.i.32–33). And he thinks he can impress Celia by offering her rare gifts and pleasures which no one else has experienced (III.vii.191–217).

Mosca shows the same desire to be exceptional. We saw how, in his soliloquy at the start of Act III, he rejects the role of an ordinary parasite (the common type described in classical literature who aims at free dinners) and claims that the 'true' parasite is something divine: 'dropped from above, / Not bred 'mongst clods, and clotpoles, here on earth.' His pure skill makes him feel like a spirit freed from the body ('I could skip / Out of my skin'). Really, of course, Mosca is not all spirit, but all mind, all intelligence. Apart from his quick-wittedness he has almost no character. He fails with Bonario and Celia because he has no moral sense which could make him capable of understanding how good people will behave in an emergency. Among people like himself, he never fails when he is exercising his pure skill in manipulation. But at the end he does fail with Volpone because he is no longer practising his skill for its own sake. He is applying it to the cruder purpose of getting rich and becoming a gentleman.

The three 'birds of prey' are designed as a group—the smart career-lawyer, the decrepit old father, the jealous young husband—quite different types united by greed, so that each one gives up what he values most for the sake of Volpone's money. But within that design their separate characters are sharply realised. **Corvino** has the longest and most complex part, which will be discussed in Part 4. **Voltore**, throughout the play, is treated ironically as a shrewd man of the world. In his first scene, Mosca begins by praising his 'wise' policy of keeping Volpone's favour by arriving early and bringing gifts (I.iii.3–6). His bedside manner is professionally smooth ('Would to heaven, / I could as well give health to you, as that plate'), but he suddenly loses his smoothness and becomes excited when Mosca whispers 'You are his heir.' Pretending not to notice his excitement, Volpone and Mosca then start to talk piously about death, so that Voltore has to force the conversation back to the subject which interests him. We noticed similar teasing when Mosca obliges him to listen to his insulting speech about lawyers (see above, p. 17). Mosca's technique with Voltore is to play continually on his image of himself as a worldly-wise lawyer, while showing how gullible his greed makes him. Thus in three separate scenes (I.iii; III.ix; V.xii) we see his doubts and suspicions overcome by an assurance that Volpone and Mosca are plotting for his benefit.

Corbaccio, by contrast, is so deaf and blind that he is hardly aware of what is going on around him, yet he clings tenaciously to his greedy purpose. He is so old that the only thing he could hope to do with Volpone's wealth is to bequeath it to his son, whom he none the less disowns in order to get it. As was mentioned before, Corbaccio's age makes him impatient to get results quickly (see III.ix.14). Unconscious of how he appears to others, he is open in showing his selfish cruelty and grasping miserliness (see I.iv.40–80). In this way Jonson sternly prevents us from feeling sorry for him. Instead we are shown an aged sinner as a horrible and painfully ridiculous sight.

The ridiculousness of **Sir Politic** and **Lady Would-Be**, and their function in Jonson's design, has already been discussed (see comments on II.i; III.iv; IV.i). Their characters are mainly revealed through floods of foolish chatter. Notice also, however, that in spite of their social rank and pretensions they are both shown as basically 'vulgar' characters. For example, St Mark's Cathedral—symbol of the Venetian culture which Sir Pol professes to admire so much—is the spot where he chooses to urinate (IV.i.144). And his wife, who models herself on the cultured ladies of Italian courts, offers her body not only to Volpone but also, it appears, to his servant (V.iii.40–43). Of all the play's characters **Peregrine** is the least well-defined. Jonson needs him mainly as someone for Sir Pol to talk to. His role is best explained through the theory that the English characters are also involved in an animal fable (see the article by Jonas A. Barish cited below in 'Suggestions for further reading'). 'Pol' is a common English name for a parrot, a bird which not only chatters but imitates. Thus the Would-Bes, as well as being parrot-like by talking so much, are also parrot-like by foolishly trying to imitate Italian vices. Peregrine's name, though Greek for 'traveller', is also the name of a kind of hawk which chases small birds. This helps to explain that his function in the play is to reveal and finally to punish the parrot's folly.

Most readers complain that **Celia** and **Bonario** are dull characters. This is true up to a point, but we must understand why Jonson made them as they are. He certainly meant them to remind his audience of Virtue-figures in Morality drama, who had none of the theatrically-exciting qualities of the Vices. Also, in line with his theory that the theatre always tends to make vice more attractive than virtue, he deliberately insists that his virtuous characters must be judged by moral, not theatrical, standards. He makes Celia's simple innocence contrast with her husband's complex viciousness, and her unchanging constancy contrast with Volpone's role-playing. Bonario's directness is opposed to Mosca's devious scheming; his unselfish behaviour toward Celia is opposed to his father's selfishness. There are also, however, subtler ways in which Jonson uses these characters. In the first place, Celia is a sexually-attractive woman, 'a beauty, ripe, as harvest!' Unless we are very pure ourselves, we may be tempted to think that she is wasted on a man like Corvino and would do better with Volpone. Though she asks us to believe that her beauty is a misfortune, not every man in the audience will agree. Her sex-appeal is another of the traps which Jonson sets for our moral judgement. In Bonario's case the trap is quite different. We are tempted to accept him too easily as an effective champion of virtue. We may be thrilled when he leaps to the rescue of Celia like a knight in a medieval romance, but should we really believe that vice in Machiavelli's Europe can be defeated by old-fashioned chivalry? The problem with Bonario, and to some extent Celia, is that they don't have enough of the worldly wisdom which their persecutors have too much of. We know more than they do about the people they suffer from and the world they live in. During the second half of the play, they stand side by side in the dock, helplessly protesting their innocence and praying to heaven for protection. In the end their prayers are answered, but if we suppose their goodness has overcome evil, we are finding a comfort which the play does not provide.

Imagery

Images are the elements in a work of literature which influence our imaginations to look at life in a particular way. They are the details which build up the 'vision' of life which the author communicates to us.

Images in drama are mostly of two kinds: visual and verbal. Visual images are liable to be forgotten when we read a play, but they have the strongest impact in the theatre. Our first sight of Volpone kneeling before his treasure is a visual image of his gold-worship. His disguises— his changes of costume and appearance—are visual images of his deceitfulness and delight in role-playing. Stage-furniture can also provide visual images: the mountebank's platform in II.ii emphasises Volpone as 'actor'; and his bed, prominent in so many scenes, also emphasises his 'sickness' and his lust for Celia. An extreme example of a visual image is the tortoise-shell (V.iv). Sir Pol, who has earlier showed his folly entirely through his words, finally shows it visually (and silently) as he creeps round the stage in his ridiculous hiding-place.

Usually, of course, visual imagery is reinforced by words, and verbal images are often made to work on our imagination without reference to anything visible on stage. Volpone's opening speech provides examples. The visual image of the kneeling worshipper is verbally reinforced when Volpone at once calls his treasure-chest a 'shrine' and his treasure a 'saint'. Then he begins to use imaginative language (metaphors, comparisons) to explain his religion further. He calls gold 'the world's soul, and mine,' denying the usual distinction between spiritual and material, claiming that for him and the rest of the world gold, not the soul, is the most precious of possessions. He tells us that he is more glad to see his treasure than the earth is glad to see the sun in spring: holding up a gold coin (line 10), he says it is brighter than the sun.

These sun-references stress his blasphemy and unnaturalness, since the sun in Jonson's time was an image of God's rule in the universe. the first thing he made when he created the world out of chaos (lines 8 10) to bring life to nature and regulate its course. Volpone next turns to an image out of literature, the poetic concept of 'the golden age' (lines 14–16), taking it literally and pretending that the poets had meant that the best age would be one of materialism. What they actually meant by the golden age was a world of perfect happiness, an impossible ideal, but Volpone argues that his gold makes perfect happiness possible. For him, it is the hope of finding happiness in human relationships that is an impossible ideal, or 'waking dream' (line 18). He throws in another literary image in his reference to 'golden' Venus (line 19), preparing us for the connection to be made in the play between gold and sex. But the climax of his speech is the image of wealth as the 'dumb god':

> Riches, the dumb god, that giv'st all men tongues;
> That canst do nought, and yet mak'st men do all things;
> The price of souls; even hell, with thee to boot,
> Is made worth heaven!

Twisting the simple proverb 'silence is golden,' Volpone describes gold as a god who says and does nothing himself but can make men say and do anything, even sell their souls. Much of the play will illustrate this image. We see here, incidentally, that Volpone admits the existence of the soul, and of heaven and hell, but thinks that to be rich and damned is better than to be virtuous and poor.

So it is mainly through images that Jonson shocks us into awareness of Volpone's upside-down values in that opening 'hymn'. In the rest of the play images of wealth and luxury keep recurring, including the visual ones of Voltore's gold plate, Corbaccio's bag of coins, Corvino's jewels, and the rope of pearl which Volpone offers to Celia. Gold, to its devotees, has the magical power of the alchemist's elixir: to cure the sick (I.iv.71–72), to increase sexual powers (III.vii.217), to make the old and ugly attractive:

> *It is the thing*
> *Makes all the world her grace, her youth, her beauty.*
>
> (V.ii.104–5)

Rich men have a habit of using their money to buy the bodies of beautiful women. Although sex is not the greatest of Volpone's pleasures, the link between his gold-worship and his sexual greed is made clear when Mosca tells him about Celia:

> *O, sir, the wonder,*
> *The blazing star of Italy! a wench*
> *O' the first year, a beauty, ripe, as harvest!*
> *Whose skin is whiter than a swan, all over!*
> *Than silver, snow, or lillies! a soft lip*
> *Would tempt you to eternity of kissing!*
> *And flesh that melteth, in the touch, to blood!*
> *Bright as your gold! and lovely as your gold!* (I.v.107–14)

The imagery is well-calculated to appeal to Volpone. The woman is a 'blazing star' (that is, a comet, something exceptional, which occurs rarely); she is 'ripe, as harvest' (ready to be picked); she is white like emblems of purity (thus fit to be corrupted); her lip would tempt him to 'eternity of kissing' (a sexual heaven). But the erotic climax—her body will melt with passion when you touch her—is followed by the most persuasive image of all to Volpone: she is as bright and lovely as his *gold*. And four lines later Mosca knows he can appeal to his master by describing Celia as someone else's 'treasure' to be stolen: 'She's kept as warily as is your gold'.

Volpone's perverted approach to sex is often shown through literary images. When he first describes his passion (II.iv.1–11), he uses images of frustrated love from the Petrarchan tradition of love-poetry which Jonson disapproved of as artificially erotic: he is wounded by Cupid's darts, shot from the woman's eyes like flames; he burns like a furnace; his liver melts; he is a heap of cinders. He goes to Roman erotic poets for his images of love-making. From Catullus he takes the image of 'theft' to describe the pleasure of secret sex (III.vii.180–3), and from Ovid the stories of the Roman gods' love-affairs which he and Celia will 'enact' (ibid.221–5). Here we find him again using images of disguise and role-playing which indicate that his idea of 'the true heaven of love' (ibid.140) is one which will satisfy his vanity, his love of himself more than his desire for Celia.

None the less, Jonson does stress his animal lust to show that greed for sex as well as gold is a sign of man's animal nature. Earlier, Volpone has feared the 'hell' of having his 'appetite' for Celia spoiled by Lady Would-Be's visit (III.iii.27–29). Obviously, Jonson's dominating vision in *Volpone* is of men as animals. The characters themselves are images contributing to this vision by their animal names and the roles they play in the animal fable (see especially I.i.87–91; I.ii.95–97; I.iii.81; V.ii.64–68; V.v.6–9, 18; V.vi.27–28; V.viii. 11–14; V.xii.125). In a performance of the play the characters will also be *visual* images if they are made to *look* like animals. Significantly, the two characters who are not animal-istic are described as animals by those who slander them in court: Bonario is called 'swine, goat, wolf' and 'viper' by his father (IV.v.111–12), and Celia is given the names of traditionally lustful animals, 'partridge' and 'jennet', by Corvino (ibid.118–19) and of traditionally untrustworthy animals, 'chameleon' and 'hyena', by Lady Would-Be (IV.vi.2–3). Jonson uses a powerful animal image to conclude the last court-scene:

> *Mischiefs feed*
> *Like beasts, till they be fat, and then they bleed.*
> (V.xii.151)

This suggests, not only that wicked men grow fat by eating their fellow-men, but also that the Venetian court sees itself as a slaughter-house, an *abattoir*.

Men behaving like animals, forgetting their souls in the pursuit of riches and pleasure, possessed by the urge to possess—this is what Jonson diagnoses as the human sickness. Images of sickness and disease, of corruption and rottenness, occur very frequently. We have noted many of them already in this book. It would be a useful exercise to collect them.

Rhetoric and irony

Like all writers trained in the classical tradition, Jonson thought of literature in terms of 'rhetoric'—the art of using language persuasively. Rhetoric was originally the art of public speaking (Greek *rhetor* meant 'speaker'), but since ancient times it had been applied to every kind of writing. The writer must identify the kind of public he means to address and then plan every word with the aim of persuading his public to accept his message. Moralists, classical as well as Christian, were well aware that the verbal skills of rhetoric could be dangerous if they were used irresponsibly or maliciously (as they are used, for example, by

Voltore in IV.v). They therefore insisted that rhetoric should be used in the service of truth. In exactly what sense does *Volpone* 'serve truth'?

In earlier comedies Jonson had expressed his message openly through 'mouthpiece' characters. They triumphed over their enemies, the satirised characters, and plainly told the audience what it ought to think. Such plays showed Jonson teaching directly, using rhetoric 'straight' like a preacher, and they were not very successful because theatre-audiences do not like being preached at.

Most dramatists avoid such obvious methods of teaching and yet manage to express a point of view on the action and persuade their audience to share it. They do this by involving the audience emotionally in the story and guiding its responses. To some extent we can say that Jonson does this in *Volpone*. He makes us feel pity for Celia and disgust at Corvino, for example. He shocks us emotionally with the harsh satiric vision of materialism and animalism we have just been studying. Certainly *one* aim of Jonson's rhetoric is to make us aware of dangerous truths about human nature and to warn us to be on our guard against them.

But in the course of this book it has been suggested many times that Jonson's role in *Volpone* is more that of a tempter than a guide. He tempts us to enjoy Volpone and Mosca instead of condemning them, and tempts us to laugh at things which are despicable rather than amusing. Possibly he tempted his audience at the Globe to take a wrong view of Celia's sexual attractiveness and a wrong view of the Would-Bes' folly. Certainly he cheats us if we hope that Bonario and Celia will emerge triumphant as hero and heroine, and if we trust that the court will be a model of wisdom and Christian justice. These deceptions are difficult to reconcile with the theory that a writer should guide his public to a perception of truth.

Jonson's method can be explained by relating it to a particular kind of rhetoric which was widely practised by serious writers in his day—by Spenser, for example, in *The Faerie Queen* and by Milton in *Paradise Lost*. Instead of merely *showing* their readers the truth, they challenged them to find the truth for themselves, and often made it difficult for them to do so. Just as the Christian life was often described as a battleground, where every individual had to fight against the devil's temptations, so the *experience* of a work of literature could be made a kind of trial, a controlled rehearsal for the battle of life, in which the reader's moral judgement could be tested and trained. This deceptive rhetoric was justified by the Christian belief that temptation was valuable if it strengthened the mind to resist falsehood and hold firmly to the truth. In applying it to drama, Jonson had the example before him of medieval morality plays, which, as we saw, had tempted audiences to find vice more amusing than virtue. And he found the method particularly helpful because it enabled him to reconcile his distrust of the theatre with his desire to write successful plays. By using the false attractions of the theatre as bait for his hook, he was able to please and to educate his public at the same time.

Jonson is therefore an ironic dramatist in the sense that he conceals his real purpose from his audience. It is interesting to notice the parallel between *his* irony and the irony practised by characters in the play. They, too, are continually tempting and deceiving each other. We are reminded of this by images. Volpone talks of tempting his clients by 'letting the cherry knock against their lips' (I.i.89). He compares his delusive tricks to those of the 'fox / Mocking a gaping crow' (I.ii.95–97). His gold is a 'bait' which 'covers any hook' (I.iv.135), and he later tempts Celia with 'sensual baits' (III.vii.210). Mosca prepares a 'trap' for his master (V.v.18), who also makes a 'snare' for his own neck (V.xi.1). Deceptive rhetoric is practised throughout most of the play, though the biggest examples of it are the mountebank's sales-talk and Voltore's speech in the law-court. The *difference* between Jonson's deceptive irony and that of his characters is of course one of motive— their motives are selfish while his is supposedly educational.

Did Jonson really believe that he could educate his public in this way? The last words of the play suggest that he was doubtful. In the Epilogue, Volpone steps forward to address the audience and ask for applause. He hopes that, although he has been punished by the laws of Venice, spectators will not feel that he has committed any crime ('fact') against them. By applauding, he says, they will acquit him. Maintaining his irony to the end, Jonson assumes that the spectators' applause will show that they have enjoyed his play as 'good theatre' and ignored its moral relevance to themselves.

The idea that a writer of comedy should approach his audience in a critical and even hostile spirit may seem strange to some readers, especially those who are accustomed to the more good-natured comedies of Shakespeare. But those who are familiar with present-day theatre may find links between *Volpone* and the so-called 'black comedies' of writers such as Beckett, Ionesco, Pinter and Albee. Such writers also resent the assumption that comedy should provide easy relaxation, and they aim to make spectators feel challenged and uncomfortable when they laugh. This link may be one of the reasons why *Volpone* is so often acted today.

Part 4

Hints for study

Reading the play

It is advisable to read the play at least *three* times, leaving several days between each reading:

(*i*) a quick reading, ignoring problems of language as far as possible. Aim to become familiar with the story, to enjoy the humour of the situations, and to visualise the fast-moving action. Use the general summary and the scene-by-scene summaries in Part 2.

(*ii*) a slow, patient reading, making sense of each line, looking up difficult words and allusions in the glossary of your edition. This is hard work, but absolutely essential for full understanding.

(*iii*) a critical reading. If your second reading has been careful, this will be the most interesting and enjoyable stage. You will now feel at home with Jonson's language, and able to form your own ideas of what he is saying and doing. Use Part 3, noting where you agree or disagree with what is said, and making additional notes from your own experience.

At this final stage you may have to prepare for an exam. The following hints are meant to help you to do so. Preparing for an essay is in most respects similar.

Preparing for examinations

Organising your material

To write a good examination answer it is not quite enough to know the play well and be interested in it; you must also have facts and ideas arranged clearly in your mind so that you can draw on them quickly, as needed. It is not a good idea to prepare answers in advance, since you are not likely to be asked the questions you have prepared for. The best examination answers *adapt* prepared material to the demands of the question.

You could arrange your material under the headings used in Part 3, but do not simply memorise what is there. Under *themes*, for example, try to find your own examples and illustrations of the themes we considered. And be ready to find others. For example, it was only in the section on 'Rhetoric and irony' that we discovered the theme of temptation.

A clear idea of the *structure and pattern* of the play is essential. How do the fortunes of Volpone and Mosca rise and fall? (You could prepare this in the form of a graph). What are the main climaxes in the action? Is it significant that Acts I, III and V open with soliloquies? Why do Volpone's disguises show him alternating between passive and active roles? Do you think that certain scenes are designed to contrast with each other?

Characters: before considering individual characters, see how they are grouped (Volpone, Mosca and the 'family' / The three 'birds of prey' / Bonario and Celia / the Would-Bes and Peregrine / the judges). Then be prepared to differentiate between the characters in each group. Volpone and Mosca work mainly as a team, but are they good at different things? Do they differ in their motives? How does Jonson achieve variety between the parallel roles of Voltore, Corbaccio and Corvino? Are Bonario and Celia mere symbols of goodness, or do they have any characteristics that make them individual? Though Sir Politic and Lady Would-Be are both foolish, does their folly take different forms? Why are they in Venice? And what is each one most interested in?

Preparing for a question on *imagery*, it is necessary to make lists (for example, under animals, gold, sex, disease, disguise, temptation). Here again, try to find your own examples: take note of them as you read. Remember also that the meaning and effectiveness of an image depends on the context in which it is used. So be ready to explain this. (To say that Celia is described as a chameleon would be true, but you must also explain that this image of an animal which changes colour to suit its surroundings is inappropriate to Celia and ironically appropriate to Lady Would-Be who uses it).

The subject of *irony* is central in *Volpone* and sometimes difficult to discuss. To think clearly on the subject keep the following definition in mind. 'Irony is a secret which A *shares* with B and *conceals* from C.' As you revise, apply this formula to particular situations. What is the secret? Who shares it? Who is deceived? For example, in I.iii, when the lawyer pays his visit, the secret is that Volpone is not really sick, and it is shared by Volpone and Mosca at the expense of Voltore. This irony is made stronger by the fact that Voltore thinks that he and Mosca are deceiving Volpone. Usually the characters share their secret with the audience. You should also look for the kind of irony which is concealed from the characters and is shared with the audience by the author; and finally for the kind of irony which the author conceals from everyone but challenges the audience to detect. (The writer of this book has argued that the second of these last two kinds of irony is more common than the first, but you may not agree with him).

Quotations

These are effective in persuading an examiner that you know the play well. But it is important to know how to use them. If you find it easy, you could memorise long passages (4–10 lines), but do not quote such passages unless you mean to analyse them fully. On page 55, the quotation of Mosca's 8-line description of Celia was justified because comments were made on almost every line. But to quote such a passage *without* full analysis would merely show the examiner that you have a good memory and would not impress him very much.

Shorter quotations, even single lines or phrases, are much more effective. In revising, make a note of passages which illustrate characters and themes and memorise them *accurately*. Notice how they are used in the specimen answers which follow.

Comparisons

Although your main task is to show detailed understanding of *Volpone*, you should also try to see the play in a wider perspective. Make use of any knowledge you have of other comedies in English or other literatures. The comparison between Jonson's and Shakespeare's comedies is always fruitful, provided you make clear that the two dramatists were trying to do different things. If you happen to know Shakespeare's *The Merchant of Venice*, you could consider 'Venice' as a symbol of wealth in both plays and make interesting contrasts between the attitudes of Shylock and Volpone to money, between the trial-scenes, and between the aims and methods of satiric and romantic comedy.

Answering examination questions

General advice

Read the question carefully, think about it, and take time to make an outline plan of your answer before you start to write. Do not try to put down everything you know. Examiners are interested in the intelligence you show in answering the question, not in how much you write. They will penalise irrelevance, bad logic, and poor design.

There is no 'right' answer to a question on literary criticism. The following specimen-answers are meant as a guide to *method*. Different, and better, answers can easily be imagined.

A question on themes

Question 1. *How does the opening scene of* Volpone *serve to introduce Jonson's themes in the play?*

ADVICE: Start with a brief description of the scene and then show how the themes grow out of it. This is more logical than to begin by listing themes.

OUTLINE: Brief account of opening scene
           Volpone's hymn: gold-worship
           Volpone and Mosca: Volpone's vanity; Mosca as
              manipulator
           Volpone's soliloquy: greed and temptation
           Brief conclusion

SPECIMEN ANSWER:

The scene is in three parts: first Volpone's hymn to his gold; then a conversation between Volpone and his servant Mosca; finally, after Mosca has been sent to summon the dwarf, the eunuch and the hermaphrodite, Volpone tells the audience about his method of getting rich.

The main theme of the play is introduced in the first line: 'Good morning to the day; and, next, my gold!' The play pictures a society which worships money, and we are prepared for this by our first sight of Volpone, who calls his treasure-chest a 'shrine' and his gold a 'saint'. When he hails gold as 'the world's soul,' he implies that his religion is not just personal but universal. Reversing the Christian belief that spirit is higher than matter, he suggests that his priorities are those which men really follow, as opposed to those which they profess. Like Machiavelli, he is more interested in what men actually do than in what they should do. The play will support his claim that people value money above personal relationships and will do anything to get it.

The conversation with Mosca introduces new ideas. One is that Volpone is not an ordinary miser. He takes less delight in being rich than in finding clever ways of becoming rich ('I gain no common way'). This desire to be exceptional and to avoid everything 'common' was a mark of the Renaissance nobleman; but we see it later as a sign of Volpone's vanity. The other thing we see here is how Mosca flatters his master and manipulates him into giving him a gift. This is a foretaste of how Mosca will take advantage of Volpone's vanity in Act V.

The main themes which emerge from Volpone's soliloquy are greed and temptation. He shows his own greed for pleasure when he asks 'What should I do, / But cocker up my genius and live free / To all delights my fortunes call me to?' But the pleasure he describes lies in exploiting the cruder greed of his clients. He presents himself as a deceitful tempter, 'letting the cherry knock against their lips'. All through the play, Volpone and Mosca will not only tempt their victims but will also tempt the audience to applaud their villainy.

Though the themes are very serious, it is clear from this opening scene that Jonson means to present them in a deceptively amusing way.

A question on character-relationship

Question 2. *Discuss the changing relationship between Volpone and Mosca in* Volpone.

ADVICE: There are many ways of approaching this question. But if you start at the beginning and work through the play scene-by-scene, you may leave yourself no time for the important scenes in Act V. Better to focus on the *breakdown* of the relationship and show how this has been prepared for in earlier scenes.

OUTLINE: Summary of the relationship
The breakdown: Volpone's mistake; Mosca's mistake
A surprise, but prepared for earlier
Thematic significance

SPECIMEN ANSWER:
Volpone describes a partnership between two rogues, master and servant. Each using the other's talents, they achieve amazing successes. Even when they face disaster at the end of Act III (when Bonario rescues Celia), they are able to combine to achieve a still greater triumph in the law-court (where Bonario and Celia are convicted). Ultimately, however, they turn against each other and both are destroyed.

The most significant change in their relationship occurs in Act V. At the start of it, they are congratulating each other much as they did in Acts I and II. Volpone praises Mosca's art as a manipulator ('Exquisite Mosca!') and Mosca flatters his master on his skill as an actor. 'This is our masterpiece,' says Mosca, 'We cannot think, to go beyond this.' But a few lines later we find him tempting his master to go further. And after the scene of the clients' disappointment it becomes clear that Mosca has seen his opportunity as 'the heir' and is encouraging his master to leave him in charge of the house.

Going out into the street to tease his victims, the fox becomes the stinging fly. In doing this Volpone indulges his vanity, his enjoyment of another disguise and his appetite for cruel laughter. He is not suspicious of Mosca, because it is part of his vanity to assume that his servant depends on him. But Mosca also underestimates Volpone. When he appears in the law-court dressed as a gentleman—the fly has become the fox—he does not understand that Volpone (who really is 'by blood, and rank a gentleman') will have too much pride to let his servant destroy him.

This breakdown in their relationship is surprising enough to make a strong dramatic climax, but it is not so surprising as to be inconsistent with the earlier action. Ever since the first scene, where Mosca flatters Volpone into giving him a present, we have suspected that he was the cleverer of the two, waiting for his opportunity. On the other hand, we have also guessed that Volpone believed that it was a gentleman's privilege to receive flattery and give presents, and that he would never allow Mosca to take his place.

When Voltore, Corbaccio and Corvino are persuaded to work together to get Volpone acquitted, Jonson shows us an extreme example of partnership depending on self-interest. The partnership of Volpone and Mosca is essentially similar. In both Jonson satirises the only kind of 'society' possible where greed and individualism rule. He suggests that such a society cannot be destroyed by 'goodness' (Bonario and Celia) or 'justice' (the court), but falls apart internally and destroys itself.

A question on a character's place in the design of the play

Question 3. *Discuss the role of Corvino in the design of* Volpone.

ADVICE: This is a common type of question focusing on a minor character with a significant role in the play. You should aim, not so much to describe the character, as to show how the author uses him in his total design.

OUTLINE: Summary of Corvino's role in the plot
Moral significance of his role: greed overcoming sexual honour; unconscious hypocrisy
Significance of his punishment: folly; ignorance of the self; shamelessness

SPECIMEN ANSWER:
Corvino, the merchant, differs from the other two 'birds of prey' by having something apart from his money which Volpone wants. He guards his wife Celia jealously, keeps her watched at home by spies,

and in Act II chastises the mountebank for daring to speak to her. Yet to win Volpone's favour he will urge his wife to go to bed with him, and later in the law-court, to ensure Volpone's acquittal, he will publicly denounce his wife as a whore and proclaim himself a cuckold.

Thus, like the other clients, he is used by Jonson to show that greed is the strongest of human obsessions. For the sake of Volpone's money he sacrifices what seemed to be the most important thing in his life, his 'honour' as a husband. In Volpone's bedroom he even tells Celia, hypocritically, that honour is 'a mere term / Invented to awe fools'.

But the point which Jonson stresses about Corvino's hypocrisy is that he is never aware of it. In spite of the awful things he does, he always thinks of himself as a 'good Catholic', a man of 'conscience' and 'scruple'. In Act I he believes that his pity for Volpone is sincere (''Las, good gentleman! / How pitiful the sight is!'), and Mosca has to persuade him to show his true feelings by shouting abuse into Volpone's ear when he is sure that Volpone cannot hear him. He is genuinely horrified when Mosca suggests stifling the old man, but he is willing to let Mosca go ahead provided he takes the responsibility. His sadistic cruelty reappears when he bullies Celia in Act II, and in the law-court he so enjoys abusing Celia that he scandalises the court. Yet he still asks Mosca to reassure him that 'there is no shame in this, now, is there?'

Shame is a key-word in respect of Corvino. As Volpone points out, he sings his shame aloud, like the crow in the fable, but his last words in the play are 'I shall not see my shame, yet'. His punishment is to be rowed round Venice wearing ass's ears. This symbol of folly does not mean that Jonson takes a lenient view of Corvino. On the contrary, Jonson is showing us how closely vice and folly are connected. Corvino's folly is ignorance of himself, of his own true nature. This folly makes him incapable of shame and therefore capable of the most vicious behaviour.

A question on the nature of comedy

Question 4. *In the Dedication of* Volpone *Jonson defends the harsh ending of his play on the ground that comedy should 'imitate justice, and instruct to life'. In what sense does the last scene of* Volpone *do this? And what kind of comedy results?*

ADVICE: This is a more abstract question than the previous ones, asking you to consider Jonson's theory of comedy and the unusual kind of comedy which *Volpone* represents. Try, however, not to generalise too much; show detailed knowledge of the play where you can.

OUTLINE: Why did Jonson need to defend the ending?
How does it 'imitate justice'? The punishments are appropri-
ate, but is this perfect justice?
How does it 'instruct to life'? Directly? Indirectly?
The Epilogue as a clue to the nature of the comedy

SPECIMEN ANSWER:
The Dedication of *Volpone* was written after the play and is a statement
of literary theory, not necessarily a reliable guide to the author's practice. None the less, we must believe Jonson when he says that he deliberately made his play end differently from most comedies. He knew that
English, as well as classical, comedies almost always ended joyfully.
Shakespeare's, for example, usually end with marriages, feasts, dances:
symbols of harmony and reconciliation which show that evil can be
converted by goodness or at least driven out and temporarily forgotten.
But *Volpone* ends with harsh punishments on five characters (two
others, the Would-Bes, have already been humiliated). Celia is to be
sent home to her father, and we are not allowed to think that she will be
free to marry Bonario. The play ends with no suggestion of hope for a
better future.

Jonson tells us that his aim was to answer the objection that vice was
never punished in comedy. The punishments in *Volpone* could be said
to 'imitate justice' in the sense that they are appropriate to the crimes
committed. Voltore is dismissed from the profession he has disgraced;
Corbaccio is to learn how to die in a monastery; Corvino's folly is to
be publicly exposed. Mosca, who has masqueraded as a gentleman, is
to receive the punishment of a commoner—to be whipped and sent to
the galleys—and Volpone, who has got rich by pretending to be sick, is
to be kept in prison until he is 'sick . . . indeed'. But these punishments,
however appropriate, cannot be said to represent justice in its ideal
Christian form. The court has been shown as too gullible and corruptible to serve as a perfect model. Moreover, it has ignored Celia's plea
for mercy, which (as Portia in Shakespeare's *The Merchant of Venice*
reminds us) was a necessary ingredient of justice in the Christian
scheme.

If even the judges are meant to be criticised, how does Jonson teach
in *Volpone*? By 'instruct to life' he means that comedy should teach us
how to live better lives. The leading judge tells us that we can learn about
vice from studying examples of it, and no doubt it was a part of Jonson's
purpose in *Volpone* to teach through examples of vice and virtue. But it
is hard to feel that Jonson aimed to teach so directly. The severe con-
demnation of Volpone and Mosca in the last scene shocks us into

realising that for most of the play we have been laughing along with them and enjoying their cleverness. Then, when Volpone speaks the Epilogue, he reminds us that in the theatre we always acquit criminals who have amused and entertained us. The whole play has been tempting us to enjoy as 'good theatre' what we ought to condemn in real life. The kind of comedy Jonson offers is closer to the 'black comedies' of the twentieth century than to the comedies of Shakespeare. In making us laugh it challenges us to think about whether we should be laughing at all.

Part 5

Suggestions for further reading

The text

For a list of editions of *Volpone* (all of which contain useful critical introductions) see *A note on the text* in Part 1 (p. 11). The text followed in this book is Ben Jonson, *Volpone*, edited by Philip Brockbank, The New Mermaids, Ernest Benn Limited, London, 1968.

Other works by Ben Jonson

Selected plays:
  Every Man in his Humour, 1598, revised 1616
  Sejanus, 1603
  Epicoene, or The Silent Woman, 1609
  The Alchemist, 1610
  Bartholomew Fair, 1614
  The Devil is an Ass, 1616

Poetry:
JONSON, BEN: *Poems*, edited by Ian Donaldson, Oxford University Press, London, 1975
JONSON, BEN: *The Complete Poems*, edited by George Parfitt, Penguin Books, Harmondsworth, 1975 (also contains an edition of Jonson's critical work, *Discoveries*, and his *Conversations with William Drummond*)

General reading

BAMBOROUGH, J.B., *Ben Jonson*, Hutchinson University Library, Hutchinson, London, 1970. A good general study of Jonson.
BARISH, JONAS A., 'The Double Plot in *Volpone*', *Modern Philology*, LI, 1953, pp.83–92. Also contained in the next item.
BARISH, JONAS A., editor, *Volpone: A Casebook*, Casebook Series, The Macmillan Press, London, 1972. A very useful collection of critical essays and comments on the play.

KNIGHTS, L.C., *Drama and Society in the Age of Jonson*, Chatto & Windus, London, 1937. A classic study of the sociological background to Jacobean drama.

LEGGATT, ALEXANDER, *Ben Jonson: his vision and his art*, Methuen, London, 1981. Excellent on Jonson as a whole.

PARTRIDGE, EDWARD B., *The Broken Compass: A Study of the Major Comedies of Ben Jonson*, Chatto & Windus, London, 1958. Contains the best study of imagery in *Volpone*.

The author of these notes

DOUGLAS DUNCAN was educated at Corpus Christi College, Oxford, and holds a Ph.D. from the University of Aberdeen. He has been Lecturer in English at the University of Southampton, Professor of English at the University of Ghana, and is now Professor of English at McMaster University, Hamilton, Ontario. His publications include books on Scottish and American literature and an edition of Ben Jonson's *Bartholomew Fair*. His *Ben Jonson and the Lucianic Tradition* was published by Cambridge University Press in 1979.